John Clarke practised as a litigation solicitor for 44 years, beginning as an articled clerk in Westminster and later working in Brighton, King's Lynn, and Wisbech. He specialised in criminal law and prison law for 37 of those 44 years. Additionally, he managed an 18-acre smallholding while maintaining his legal practice.

Dedicated to all those who are part of these narratives and to those who had faith enough in my first book to buy it and, of course, to my wife, Marilyn, who patiently read the proofs and put up with my worries and elations in equal measure.

John Clarke

MORE NARRATIVES FROM "THE LAW AND I"

Austin Macauley Publishers

LONDON • CAMBRIDGE • NEW YORK • SHARJAH

Copyright © John Clarke 2025

The right of John Clarke to be identified as author of this work has been asserted by the author in accordance with sections 77 and 78 of the Copyright, Designs and Patents Act 1988.

All rights reserved. No part of this publication may be reproduced, stored in a retrieval system, or transmitted in any form or by any means, electronic, mechanical, photocopying, recording, or otherwise, without the prior permission of the publishers.

Any person who commits any unauthorised act in relation to this publication may be liable to criminal prosecution and civil claims for damages.

The story, experiences, and words are the author's alone.

A CIP catalogue record for this title is available from the British Library.

ISBN 9781035866977 (Paperback)
ISBN 9781035866984 (ePub e-book)

www.austinmacauley.com

First Published 2025
Austin Macauley Publishers Ltd®
1 Canada Square
Canary Wharf
London
E14 5AA

I would like to thank Dr Emma Nottingham, head of the Legal Department of Winchester University, for supporting me in promoting my first book; that support encouraged me to write this second book.

Table of Contents

1. Getting a Flat Before Starting in a Solicitor's Office	15
2. Views on My Articles and Apprenticeship	18
3. Inspecting a Deserted House	21
4. Mistakes Made Early on	24
5. Early Divorces	30
6. Who Is Holding the Fort when the Solicitor Is at Court?	33
7. Site Visits	36
8. Police Station Procedure	39
9. Probation	42
10. Acting for Parents and My Son	45
11. Legal Aid	47
12. The Franchise	49
13. Terrifying Judges	51
14. Two Famous Judges	56
15. Magistrates	58

16. Going to Court and the Smallholding	61
17. Countryside Crime	64
18. Prison Law	69
19. Prisons and Farm Animals	71
20. Prisoners and Pleading for Them	73
21. Shocking Videos	76
22. First Cases at Brighton	79
23. Left-Wing Attitudes	82
24. Cases Under New Case Law. New Aggravating and Mitigating Features	84
25. Clever Crooks	87
26. A Sad Case That Might Not Have Been a Crime	90
27. Stand-Off on Mother's Day	93
28. Fraternisation Between Barristers, Judges and Solicitors	95
29. Past and Future Communications in Litigation	98
30. Mothers and Their Sons in Trouble	100
31. How Murderers Behave	102
32. The Most Common Crime-Shoplifting	104
33. Paedophiles	107
34. Evidence by Identification	110
35. If You Lose a Case, Should You Resign, Like Sportsmen Do?	113

36. Reading Law Books; Looking up the Law	115
37. A Rape Case and My Brother	118
38. Serendipity in the Legal Family	120
39. How I Got Paid Over the Years	122
40. Advising Even After I've Retired!	125
41. The Law, Lawyers and Activists	128
42. New Ways to Get Legal Advice and Representation	130
43. My Reputation as a Lawyer	132
44. The Law and Practice of the New Morality—The Environment and Climate Change	134
45. Closing Courts	137
46. Technology in Solicitors' Offices Over 44 Years	139
47. How Can I Give a Picture of What the Legal Social Culture Was at the Time?	141

"A fascinating insight into the life of a remarkable legal professional, bringing unique stories from the law and beyond."

– Emma Nottingham

Other books written by the Author

The law and I published by Austin Macauley
Smallholder's & Farmer's legal handbook published by Smallholder Practical series

1. Getting a Flat Before Starting in a Solicitor's Office

The story of starting my career in law is not complete without recounting the narrative of my wife and I setting up in a flat before starting my first legal job.

I had told my father, a Judge at the Old Bailey, that I was going to marry my wife Marilyn and then start work at Radcliffe's, his chosen firm where I would commence my articles, a training period of 2 years after which, hopefully, I would become a solicitor.

My father was quietly horrified at my announcements on two accounts. He had envisaged my marrying a deb from the south. However, my fiancée was a shopkeeper's daughter from Lytham St Annes near Blackpool. He had never been there, being born and bred in the South of England. Secondly, it was also unheard of for an articled clerk to start as a married person… unheard of!

Before we were to be married, we had to find somewhere to live. We envisaged living in 'poverty' in a bedsit in Notting Hill Gate with a kitchen divided by a curtain in one corner of a room.

However, my wife saw an advertisement in ***The Times*** for a flat, attached to a house just outside London in Chingford.

That was miles away from the centre of London, as far as you can get. It's postcode was E. 4 but it was in the countryside, nearer to Waltham Abbey then the built-up area of the north of London. Heavens knows why we thought it was a possible place for us to live.

So, as part of our preparations for marriage, we set off one afternoon on our Honda 50cc motorbike to find this flat at Chingford. We were guided by a London map and the landlady's directions. In those days, there were no Google Maps. I drove the bike and my fiancée peered at the windswept pages of the A-to-Z sitting on the back.

We came to what seemed to be the place, which started with a large overgrown drive disappearing around a corner to a large house. Was this really where we might live? How embarrassing if it wasn't the right place or that they were very posh people.

We dumped the bike in the undergrowth near the road and pensively walked up the drive.

The front door seemed too posh to approach, heralded by a porch held up by two classical pillars. We walked around the corner of the house to the back. There was a door which seemed more approachable. We knocked on the door and waited. I peered around wondering why we had come. Surely this was not the place to start our married life less than a month away.

As I was wondering and thinking how we could sidle away, the door opened in front of us and an old lady with a rather grubby apron greeted us with a smile.

"Can we see Mrs Colclough?" my fiancée asked.

"I am her," she said with an inviting smile and ushered us in. I looked at her in disbelief.

Well, to cut a long story short, it was to be our first home. Not the big house but a flat to one side, probably once occupied by a chauffeur a long time ago. The whole place had a decrepit but nevertheless delightful air of disrepair. The flat, set back to one side of the big house, was self-contained above a garage and it had 4 rooms including a large kitchen.

This was where we were to commute from to the centre of London every day on a small scooter, I to go to Radcliffes'—a firm of solicitors in Westminster—and my wife, to some office in the West End as a secretary.

Our landlords were a delightful couple, looking older than they really were, whose two working children lived with them.

Mrs Colclough was a very capable gregarious housewife. Her grey hair was bundled in a dishevelled heap to one side of her head, and she was the person who had first greeted us and who appeared to be a resident housekeeper. Her husband wore a monocle and taught Law at the City of London College.

They were therefore delighted to have a trainee solicitor and his wife as tenants and a few weeks later, we were to see them as guests to our wedding at Lincolns Inn Hall and Chapel, where we are married and had our reception.

We have a photograph of them, him with his monocle jammed over one eye and she with a hat home-made from a lampshade perched on her bundle of grey hair shoved underneath it.

So started our married life and my law career.

2. Views on My Articles and Apprenticeship

Today, apprenticeships are far more organised than they were when I did my articles. As a graduate to qualify as a solicitor, I had to do 2 years as an Articled clerk.

So I had to go to a firm and do whatever I was told. I had no idea in fact what I would have to do but my degree gave me no preparation. Most if not all the partners, my employers, did not go to university and so they had no idea what I knew about Law.

In fact, I think trainees were thought of as a bit of a bother. The firm I went to had about 8 trainees of different intelligence, but I had to admit were of the same class, for Radcliffes' was a long established firm.

I wore a suit; in fact, it was a new suit I had bought for my honeymoon for I had married only 3 weeks beforehand.

There was a temptation by my employers to use Articled clerks as just cheap labour and we all accepted that. If there was something to deliver, then an articled clerk will deliver it; remember, there was no email or quick system of sending documents. There was no facsimile system either.

A package was given to you and off you went with your A-to-Z book in your pocket to find where the other firm of solicitors were, usually in the City of London.

I was lucky in a way for I had a motorbike so I could wend my way around the narrow streets of the city, peering upwards as I drove to find the street names and numbers. And I could charge a pound. That was a lot considering I was paid £10 a week.

No Law book passed my eyes unlike at University. I was given a file or a Precedent. One of them was a Writ; a claim with the name of a Plaintiff and Defendant on the front and I had to copy and adapt it for new Plaintiffs and Defendants. It didn't tax my brain and once I had got the hang of it and had it checked, I'd take it to a typist and ask her to type it—it was always a 'her'.

All typists were young girls and indeed my wife was also a typist working elsewhere in London. It was the most common job in offices.

I don't think I was given any sort of schedule identifying in what direction my training was going. I was in a department and then quite suddenly, after about 6 months, I was told I was moving to another department and was to be trained under a Managing Clerk. They were the backbone of the firm and did the real work. They were very approachable.

I never got near an older partner. I don't think they would know how to deal with a young trainee. It was younger partners who were lumbered with these 'wet behind the ears' students.

We got on with the girls mostly because we were of the same age. The only type of worker we came across were the brown-coated men looking like Laurel and Hardy or Morecombe and Wise in the Deeds basement.

These two had matching brown coats, the uniform in this basement. Perched on a tin box was a tray with a teapot and 2 cups, a discarded teabag and a tin full of teabags—the paraphernalia needed for these 'prison jailers' guarding dusty papers tied up with a red ribbon ensconced down here from 9 to 5—seemingly never to be released.

Down there were shelves galore like a sarcophagus but in a Dickens novel. Ranged along these shelves into the distance were black tin boxes with names painted in italic white on the front. If it was the name of a man, the full title 'Esquire' would be added to the name or the name of an ancient trust might be written there.

3. Inspecting a Deserted House

One thing sticks in my memory and has been there a long time for it happened when I was an Articled Clerk in 1970.

I must have been asked by the Probate department to visit an empty house and check it was secure. I presume the occupant had died. It was in Highgate, and I drove up to it on my motorbike, the only transport I had at the time.

I parked the bike on the road, took off my helmet and peered up at the edifice I was to inspect.

There it was, an empty building. No one was there but I had the key. It must have been a usual occurrence. An old woman or man had lived there and then moved to hospital or moved to a home and it had been left. There were no relatives nearby to check the house, so the job was given to the solicitor, to me, an articled clerk.

She or he may have even died suddenly in the house.

I approached the front door with trepidation. The garden was overgrown for it was late summer. No one had been around to tend the plants and cut back the brambles. A bramble had crept across the front door, so I carefully pushed it to one side. I had to find the keyhole; there it was with an early morning spiderweb stretched across it in the hope of catching a fly.

I pushed the key in; it found its way and I turned it. It worked and the catch clicked. I was not a trespasser then!

The door was stiff but I peered in through the opening. It is peculiar walking into the hall of a house, the last footfall before me being of a dead person. There were cobwebs hanging over a cracked picture on the mantelpiece of a group in clothes from the thirties, probably an important picture of the family at the height of its power.

It was a large house with a back staircase for servants and a big wide staircase for the family. Articles lay discarded in the front room, an old coat, an old shoe. The illness of the owner must have created an urgency for those taking her off to a nursing home or even by ambulance. How sad an ending to an old house from a different generation when there was no family left.

The dusty picture on the mantlepiece gave away the family's fame. There were the grandchildren sitting on the grass; a stern man sporting a wing collar in the centre and next to him maybe the woman sat, who was the last survivor and owner of the house.

I walked down the corridor to the kitchen, my footfall crunching on a discarded crust of mouldy bread. There were a few pots and pans lying about and a milk bottle full of mould. No servants seemed to have been around. The old woman must have looked after herself with the minimum of food using the same few pots. Maybe she boiled an egg for her lunch; maybe she was ill and struggled back to bed to keep warm... before she died or was taken away to a home. I will never know what happened, but something did happen suddenly.

I walked up the back staircase where the servants must have gone upstairs. They creaked weirdly. I came to the bedroom corridor where several of the doors were open or ajar. I peered in. All empty save for the same discarded items. Drawers open with clothes pulled out. It looked like a burglary, but the front door was locked and no windows were open or smashed. That was why the Probate partner in my employer's solicitors' firm looking after the estate had asked me to come and check everything.

Maybe the carers, ambulance men or undertakers were looking for clothes to take with her if she was alive.

I looked out of the window down to the tangled garden which must have been so well cared for when the photograph of the family was taken; yes, I could just see where in the lawn they all stood or sat cross-legged for the cameraman.

Now the grass was long like an old overgrown meadow. I felt I couldn't stay further; it was a bit depressing. I suspected the house would be pulled down eventually. I went down the main staircase to the front door and hall. That was it, all secure and the windows were jammed shut.

I walked out, pulled the front door to, it was a tight fit.

I turned the key in the lock. Goodbye, old house: I will never see you again.

I put my bike helmet on, started the engine and headed into London and to the office. It was lunchtime and I had sandwiches waiting.

4. Mistakes Made Early on

In December 1973, I became newly qualified, but I had no experience. You can go to law school and become acquainted with the law but how do you open a file and argue through the post with your opponent who is also a solicitor and may know more than you? When you have an appointment with a client, what do you ask him? It is all quite terrifying. But first things first, as a solicitor you can appear in court and no amount of law lectures tell you how to do that.

So the client brings you a summons—"Oh, that's what a summons looks like!"—I'd never seen one before.

But employers expect you to do and know everything. In my first firm, the company prosecuted for the Department of Social Security (as it was then called), i.e., trying to convict benefit claimants for defrauding the Department. I had never been taught evidence or how to conduct a case in court. Defending was easy, prosecuting was difficult. You had to prove the case *beyond a reasonable doubt*.

So my boss gave me the file and I read it. I noticed the defendant had been convicted before for fraud. Surely, I was on a winner.

So, the case came on. I was in an old magistrate's court dating back to the 18th century.

It was dark and we sat on benches around a heavy oak table.

The ancient surroundings didn't give me confidence.

I dealt as far as I could with the Prosecution case. At the back of the court, other solicitors were sitting looking bored and waiting for my case to finish. Then the Defendant went into the box. Surely this is where I could catch him out. I would be home and dry, once the court knew he had been convicted before—that was it!

I said to him, "You say you are honest in dealing with the Department."

He nodded, seeming to wonder why the question was asked.

"Is it not true you've defrauded the Department before?"

I think I'd got him. He looked worried. However, before he could answer, the clerk of the Court interposed, "I think we should adjourn."

I looked at him in a questioning way. The clerk watched the magistrates file out and when the last had gone, he turned to me. "You can't ask him that!" He sounded certain, and I was confused. The solicitors behind me woke up and were watching with interest.

Did they know something I didn't?

Well, my mind went fuzzy. I don't remember what I did and how I got out of that scrape. I grabbed the law book and skimmed through it trying to look learned, but I couldn't find the right page.

However, I was told you couldn't bring up his previous convictions. That would come in an Amendment to the law later, but not now.

I forget how the case ended or whether the defendant got convicted. My mind was confused as I walked back to the office. At least my boss would not know what had happened.

I walked into the office.

"Mr B wants to see you when you get back," the receptionist said and immediately looked down at papers in front of her; she looked embarrassed.

I saw him. The Department had rung to complain about me. My confidence was crushed. I didn't like it in this firm and nor did my boss. Months later, he wrote me a letter saying he had seen me reading a book. He gave me notice though I'm not sure what he meant.

He also seemed to be upset that I had asked him for the afternoon off because a farmer was combining my land and I wanted to be there. I think he thought I was going to be distracted by the Smallholding we had bought. He wanted me to go and I wanted to go. I did find another job and gave in my notice.

Having said that story, it was my mistake being ignorant of the law but I did excel at unusual cases. The firm had an important client who ran a Haulage firm. The Local Highway Authority wanted to pass a law forcing lorries to go on the bypass around the town rather than through it. There were objections and a Planning Inspector would come to hear objections. Of course, I employed a barrister and we lost, and lorries were forced to take the bypass.

However, in those days there was no guidance as to how to charge clients. It was up to the solicitor to judge; it depended on 6 or 7 rather vague factors including importance of the case to the client, complexity of the case and so on. I think my boss, Mr B got confused with how to implement this guidance. Solicitors never gave quotes. They mumbled when asked about costs:

"It's difficult to say."

"It depends on what happens in the case."

"Not sure; it'll be a difficult case."

...and so on and clients went away confused and too scared to pursue the matter further.

However, in this enquiry, I adopted a cricket scoreboard system. So much for letters out, so much for letters in, so much for reading papers per hour and so on. My boss looked over my shoulder at my scoring.

"That's rather clever," he commented. I was surprised he hadn't seen that system before. I had used it in my previous firm in Brighton.

Much later after I had been qualified for some years, I still made mistakes.

In my Gillick case, it was proceeding in the Court of Appeal with barristers, QCs, Mrs Gillick and her husband and numerous supporters sitting at the back.

Halfway through, suddenly one of the 3 judges said, "I don't seem to have page 20," and he headed over to his colleagues. They compared bundles, prepared by me and my secretary, a local Cambridgeshire girl.

I suddenly sat up realising the arrangement of the papers was my responsibility. I looked at the 3-man bench keenly trying to guess what the problem was.

The judges discussed matters out of earshot and then the central one announced, "We shall be adjourned for a short while," and they retired. Their papers were handed down and came into my hands.

We retreated to the back of the court, and I viewed the papers. One page was missing and that was the difficulty. I grabbed the page from my spare bundle, unsewed the offending judges' bundle, inserted the offending missing pages and sewed it up again. (They do not sew together bundles now. In fact, all legal papers used in cases are online!)

A problem like that couldn't be worse, especially in such an important case in the Court of Appeal before 3 judges.

Well, we won the case 3 to nil and I hope everyone there completely forgot about the solicitor who sewed the Judges' bundles incorrectly. I'm sure even the most expert of litigators can forget things.

I had a trial in the Magistrates' court. I had done all a Defence solicitor should do. I got a Proof of Evidence from my client who said he had another witness who would support his story. I said that was always useful and I saw the witness in the office and got him to make a statement. What he said exactly matched my client's account. I told him how to be a witness. I even practised with him like a dress rehearsal.

Later, I told him the date of the trial and where the Magistrates Court was.

"Don't be too late," I said. He followed my every instruction and nodded.

On the day of the trial, I felt confident. The client turned up and so did the witness. I forget what the case was about, but I tried to give the prosecution witnesses a hard time. Then came my client. He gave evidence quite well and I sat back, thinking that was the defence's case.

The clerk asked me if that was the Defendant's case and I nodded, sure we were going to win.

He was acquitted and I felt pleased with myself walking out of court. The client went up to his friend and said that he got off. I looked at the friend and recognised him and my heart sank. It was the witness, and I hadn't called him, horror of horrors! What was I going to tell him?

He looked at me. "When am I going to say my piece?" he asked.

I stared at him in the face, tried to look knowledgeable and learned. "Oh, you weren't required," I said, shook the client's hand and walked out of the building.

Don't trust Solicitors as far as you can throw them. They forget things just like the next man. They are only human.

5. Early Divorces

In my early days in the 1970s, when I gave up Conveyancing and started doing just litigation, appearing in court was quite common in Divorce.

That was because to get a divorce, you had to appear in court before a County Court Judge. So, I had to borrow the gown at the firm. I was too mean to buy one. I had to put my wing collar on and tabs and traipse downhill to the court in Brighton. You met your client, the petitioner who would have to give evidence in the witness box.

So I joined the crowd of solicitors robing up in the robing room. In those days, even the most junior solicitor could have the experience of an easy advocacy. Larger firms had solicitors who had a string of petitions to deal with.

You would knobble the usher and see if you could get on first or at least have your cases all heard together.

And the evidence given was identical with every solicitor.

Question: "Is your name and address…?"

Question: "Are you the petitioner?"

Question: "Were you married to so and so…" (and you recited clause one of the petition)

Question: "Can you look at this document?" (The single sheet of paper, the acknowledgement of service, is handed by the Usher to the Petitioner in the witness box.)

Question: "Do you identify the signature of the Respondent on this Acknowledgement of Service?"

Question: "Do you feel that your marriage has broken down irretrievably and you wish for a Decree Nisi of Divorce to be granted?" (That was your client's husband or wife's signature he/ she had put in the acknowledgment that he/ she didn't not intend to defend the case.)

You could almost hear the Judge's boredom in his granting of the petition Decree Nisi and so on. I think the judge granted about 20 to 30 petitions in 1 hour. It was like a factory.

In fact, in England, one Judge rebelled and said in open court in frustration that it was all ridiculous. I'm not sure what happened to him.

Of course, if you had a difficult Divorce Case defined where the Respondent defended the case, that prolonged the matter considerably; Defences and Replies had to be filed and the result could be a stalemate.

If you have a fight with your partner (they were not called partners in those days) in court, surely the marriage must have broken down. Most of those defended divorces were settled somehow. A lot of them were defended because if there were accusations of unreasonable behaviour which might be extreme, it might affect how the marriage assets were to be divided. Conduct during the marriage could be taken into account.

To me as a practitioner, all those years ago, one of the best films which illustrate the anguish of divorce and custody disputes was that of **Kramer vs Kramer,** which came out exactly at the same time as I was appearing in court in 1979. Admittedly, it was about American Divorce Courts. Nevertheless, the anguish between the parties was the same on either side of the pond that divided the two nation's courts.

6. Who Is Holding the Fort when the Solicitor Is at Court?

Most if not all my narratives are about clients, their behaviour and courtroom dramas. But the base is the office, and a lot of work happens there, both on and off duty.

Back at the office, while I'm away sits the receptionist who has to deal with clients who wander in and want to see me and then question the poor girl, asking why I am not upstairs in my office twiddling my thumbs with a clear desk just waiting for them.

They give up on the receptionist and ask to see my secretary, presuming the receptionist may be lying. Indeed, they think I might suddenly come out of hiding and get caught out.

So the secretary comes downstairs clutching the diary. In those days, there was just a paper diary in which everything was written and no online diary. She had to smile and look pleasant and helpful even if the client was breathing fire. In the early days, there were no signs demanding that:

'Insults and Abuse will not be tolerated by staff'

Quite simply, it was tolerated ending with tears by the secretary after the client had stormed out. It was understood that whatever happens, we must not upset the client for they could sack you and just wander into the other adjoining solicitors' office and abuse him or her instead.

In urgent cases, my secretary might ring me but of course, I was either in Court or at a Prison where phones were not allowed. In Prisons, you had to give up your mobile and put it in a locked cabinet.

So back at the office, you either felt elated if you won your case or dejected if you didn't. Once behind your desk, your secretary would come in either pleased to see you or tearful having had a hard day. Whatever had happened to either of you, both had to get to the same wavelength. On the whole, it was a great relief to see your clerk or secretary for they were women who by the nature of their sex gave an air of relief and composure.

Why else are all announcements in stressful places always given in the female voice?

So you arranged your mind to the calamities, viewed the diary, collected your files for the next day and that was it. If nothing happened about clients, there was always the office gossip to take in; on balance, however, litigators chose that work to get away from the claustrophobia of the office. Still it was very nice to hear it and not be the subject that was talked about.

Later when technology became more sophisticated, you did what everyone did—rush in, nodded to the staff, the reception, your secretary and your clerk, turned on your computer and viewed the miles of emails there, most of which you deleted. Then you could talk to your human compatriots in a civilised way.

Because you were not in most of the time, you were a stranger to others not in your department. It was only when the office party came along at Christmas did you realise how much of a stranger you were.

So, your own private office and close compatriots were always a haven to be treasured and valued.

7. Site Visits

Site visits by the Judge during a case could be fraught but also sometimes great entertainment. I had my first one during a dispute between a developer and a farmer, who incidentally had sold some of his land to the developer. These disputes were quite common and may still be common as boundaries were set out by conveyancers on plans with a thick coloured crayon. If you scaled up the crayon colour on the plan, it might be as wide as 5 to 10 feet and that, surprisingly, can cause litigation in court.

In my case, the farmer was on Legal Aid and the developer had to defend the case with his own money but it was *exactly* about 5 feet, the width of the boundary crayon line! In addition to get the conveyancer off the hook, there was usually a clause saying lines on a plan in the conveyance were for identification only and should not be relied on—like a red rag to a bull for lawyers in the litigation mood.

Often the Judge would require a site meeting and we had to instruct the client not to talk to the Judge—an impossible imperative. Usually, the client had given evidence and so was on oath as he walked around the site.

You then had the hilarious scrambling down garden paths and across a building site. The conversation might go something like this:

Client: "You see, your Honour (or some such phrase) that's where he (gesturing to the Developer who was trying to catch up) trespassed."

Me (behind the client) in a low voice: "Mr T, you mustn't say that; it's evidence!"

He turned around and glared at me before chasing after the coat tails of the Judge.

And of course, the Judge *was* listening. He couldn't help but do so and it really was evidence, out in the open and sometimes out of the hearing of the rest of the parties trying to catch up with the Judge and Mr T. I think my client was not such an ignorant yokel as he made out for he knew if he could bring to the Judge's attention as much of his grievances as possible in an informal way, so much the better. It might even tip the balance in his favour.

Another case where both parties were on legal aid (the taxpayer paying) was about a right of way over my client's land when the adjoining owner wanted his septic tank to be emptied. Once again about a very small bit of land. Neighbour disputes caused as much acrimony as divorce disputes.

On one occasion during the case, there was a site meeting with the solicitors and the parties and, unfortunately, one of the parties had invited the local press along. Things got heated and the neighbour tipped a bucket of water over my neighbour.

The police were not involved but the press had a field day and had something very juicy to report.

Incidentally, that case went to the Court of Appeal at great expense, on a technical legal point.

Legal aid was not only expensive to the taxpayer but also to the party who was not on legal aid. If the legally aided party lost, you could not get an order for costs against him or her—merely because he/she was on legal aid.

8. Police Station Procedure

The procedure in police stations have changed dramatically from when I first practised. The only rules, which were very vague, were the Judges' rules which applied to those kept in custody. I can't recall them now and I don't think any issues came up where I might have had to use them.

However, more noticeable than anything was the lack of tape recording of interviews. All interviews including my first murder case in 1974 were handwritten. There would be long silences in the questioning while the officer asking the question would write it down in his handwriting on Statement Proformas. I looked over his shoulder as far as I was able to see what he was going to ask.

The suspect replied and then the police questioner would then write down the gist of what was said and then read it back to the suspect. All very long-winded and probably not in as much detail was given in quickfire question and answer as is now done.

I would really like to have been able to speak to a practitioner who never knew anything but handwritten question and answer. Did he feel restricted by that procedure?

In addition, smoking was allowed. It was not forbidden, In fact one detective liked to smoke cigars and over the ceiling of the interview room hung a pall of smoke with no means of escape.

Mind you, talking of ceilings, unexpected mishaps did happen. In one case, my client was asked her name and address and suddenly a square polystyrene bit of the ceiling suddenly fell on her head! I opened another file with her name on it; a personal injury file.

In another case, my client was allergic to ink used to take fingerprints (another method now not used). She developed a rash. Another personal injury file was opened, and we negotiated damages to be paid to her. However, as is normal, it was paid 'without any admission of liability'.

There was quite a competition to get police station duty calls. The reason was that a duty call could lead to representing the client in the police station. If he or she was charged, you represented him in the court. Finally, if it was serious, you then might represent him in the Crown Court. It might even be a murder, and bingo!

Also, there was no question of going on holiday and missing calls, for every call could be a Murder. When on holiday, I would keep my mobile phone with me.

Once while I was on holiday in California, the call came through:

Dring, dring.

Me: Hello?

The caller: Are you Mr Clarke?

Me: Yes.

The caller: I have a duty case in the police station—can you take it?

Me (a moment's hesitation): Yes!

The caller: It is Mr so and so who has been arrested for assault.

I rang the police station.

Me: Hello. John Clarke here. I've had a duty call. Can you give me the details?

The police station: Yes. Mr so and so. He's been arrested for assault but was drunk so he won't be ready to be interviewed for another 6 hours. I'll ring you when we're ready. You'll be ready to go then?

Me (hesitating): Yes.

You see once you had accepted the call, it was yours. If I couldn't take it, I could ring the office and give it to my clerk to deal with, which of course I did because I was in California. On another case, I was on holiday in Israel, and I took the call when I was less ready to interrupt my holiday.

Dring, dring.

Caller: I have a duty call—are you available?

Me: Well, not quite; but I could if the police station can wait; I'm 700 miles away.

I was more honest there.

9. Probation

One of the Public Bodies I came across when dealing with Criminal Cases was the Probation Service. They wrote reports on clients who may have pleaded guilty, or been found guilty and the bench didn't feel able to sentence the client without first getting some background on the case and my client.

They were, for all intents and purposes, social workers who were very liberal and to a certain extent always supportive of my client so long as the client made at least a little attempt to impress the Probation Officer who interviewed them.

More importantly, they had to turn up on time for the appointment to the Probation Officer. It couldn't be worse for the client than to appear in front of Sentencing Magistrates with a nil report.

If a report was necessary, a client might find that for a report to be made, he might be refused bail. A probation officer could then go and see him in prison. A bad sign as to what sentence he might get. In Prison Law, Probation dealt with reports for prisoners who applied for Parole.

Peterborough Prison

If eventually the client was given a Community Sentence, you would have thought that was a real let-off and I think it was if the client narrowly avoided a prison sentence.

Indeed, I happen to **watch personally** Community Service being undertaken and it was a *doddle*. Criminal work overlooked by liberal probation officers—a holiday camp!

Once after I retired, I volunteered clearing an ancient graveyard. When my wife and I appeared there, across the gravestones was a group of workers with yellow jackets on, sitting and having a smoke, of what I'm not quite sure, but I had a feeling it wasn't legal.

They were convicted criminals doing unpaid work after their tea break. As far as the Supervising Officer, there was no sign. I asked one of the men and he replied in broken English (I believe he was Lithuanian—speaking Russian) that the Probation Officer had gone to Peterborough to supervise another gang! Meanwhile, there was a couple of non-smokers, us two, hacking away at the undergrowth, one a retired solicitor who once practised Criminal Law and the other his wife.

The competence of the service seemed no less competent when I did Prison Law. The Supervising Probation Officer would have to write a report for the Parole board in front of whom I appeared representing the client.

Often no Probation Officer appeared or there was no report; or there was a report most of which was cut and pasted from a previous report, and it was presented not by the writer (who was on leave) but another officer who couldn't answer any questions.

10. Acting for Parents and My Son

It's nice to have someone in the family who can be useful in their job. If he/she is a plumber or carpenter, they can fix your toilet or do your kitchen for free.

But in my case, my expertise never could be used for my parents or my son. My mother lived in Scotland when she died. I had no idea about Scottish law so I had to hand the winding up of her estate to a Scottish Solicitor. I however distributed the estate such as it was to myself and my sister.

My father died and I was his executor, but the will was drafted by my sister-in-law's father's firm and they wound up the estate. I just signed the papers.

Then a generation down the line, my son had a divorce. Surely, I would help him. Well, not really. I was too close to him, was not independent enough so I steered him towards a divorce solicitor in my former firm. It was very frustrating.

He was surprised at the cost of solicitors. He couldn't understand why they couldn't just quote a costs figure to do the job. After all, you go to a shop and there's the price stuck on the article. You can afford it so you buy it.

On the subject which deals with barristers and acting for friends, one narrative comes to mind.

I had a relative whose son died of a drug overdose. They wanted to be represented at an inquest and my brother rang wondering if I could instruct his daughter who was a newly qualified barrister. So it was all in the family and was a very sad case.

Of course, I could act and keep it in the family, so I sent the papers to my brother's daughter and she went to the inquest and reported back to me in due course.

The relatives, parents of the deceased, were very thankful and came to see us and invited us out to dinner even though it was the daughter barrister who had done all the work.

Still, that is an exact example of keeping something in the family at no charge to anyone in a very sad case. No—solicitors and lawyers have got it sewn up; they charge a rate per hour, per letter, per telephone call. You can't lose. My son was quite shocked at that, and I felt apologetic.

My mother-in-law made a will putting all her property in trust which lasted the whole of my wife's life. She never approached me for advice but went to a local solicitor. I wonder if he/or she really knew how cumbersome a trust would be to manage.

11. Legal Aid

Of course, some might ask how criminals can afford solicitors and barristers; after all, they most probably need lawyers more than any other class of the public.

Some then conclude that as they are criminals, they make money criminally so can afford lawyers!

Not true. Criminals are incompetent and dysfunctional, or the ones I have met were. No, Legal Aid was invented in 1949 to help criminals afford lawyers. It did an excellent job and initially it was run by the Law Society, the solicitors 'club'. Nowadays, one might be shocked at that nepotism. The solicitor's club in charge of handing out money to lawyers—what a con!

I was there when it was run by the Law Society with money given by the government. Any solicitor could apply for legal aid for a client even if the solicitor rarely practised criminal law. It was not regulated but it sort of worked. It was trusted that if a solicitor wanted to help a criminal wade through the court system, it was presumed he would go on courses to familiarise himself with that aspect of law.

However, the other practice that does not happen so much now was that solicitors would rely on counsel (a barrister) a lot more; counsel who was trained in advocacy in all walks of law. You could take the statement from the client, criminal or not, and then send all the papers to a barrister asking, "What do we do next and how do we do it."

Any firm could practice criminal law and any other law you care to mention and get paid by the government agency by Legal Aid, administered by the solicitor's club, the Law Society.

When I got legal aid for Mrs Gillick, the Law Society was managing Legal Aid as an agency for the government, and I applied to them to the local area office in Cambridge.

When she was initially refused legal aid, I advised her to appeal personally. She was a strong and persuasive character and I had confidence in her 'advocacy skills'. She did appear before the Appeal Committee, some of whom were barristers who I knew and had instructed from time to time.

She did persuade them and got legal aid to go to court.

12. The Franchise

When the Franchise was invented, I must say I had to look up the word to see what it meant. However, as I was in charge of litigation in the firm, I had to do something about it.

The Law Society was divested of managing Legal Aid and the Legal Aid Board was invented. In addition, those lawyers who wanted to practise in any type of law had to apply for a Franchise to practise that. I went on courses as we all had to do. It only applied to certain types of law where clients might want help.

They would have to apply for legal aid in the usual way and the financial eligibility criteria continued.

However, the solicitors' firms who wanted to advise the clients had to satisfy standards in their firm. We had never seen this before and it was a revolution.

One must bear in mind that all these solicitors didn't have to satisfy the clients that they practised the type of law the client wanted advice on. So long as they were insured, the partners were solicitors and they filed their accounts with the Law Society as well as inland revenue, that was it.

After all, if you didn't understand the client's problem, you just took a statement from him/her or them and sent all the papers off to a barrister. It was as simple as that.

We were given an enormous clip folder about 3 inches thick about the Franchise and what you had to do to get one. Our firms were required to pass certain tests about training file types, types of letters to be sent to clients, reviews of staff training and more.

It was a shock and a lot of firms decided to give up Legal Aid. That didn't matter to a lot of firms. The more 'conservative' firms never advised criminals in any event. Radcliffes' didn't. You could still advise on divorce but not offer legal aid for it.

The rates of pay were much lower than private rates and the latter firms initially didn't have to pass any of the tests that franchise applicants had to do. This was the start of the attack on legal aid.

Some firms failed their franchise test, some only applied for a minimal number of subjects, mainly matrimonial and crime.

Local Committees were set up consisting of several firms of solicitors centred round the geographical area of a local duty solicitor court and police station system.

I was appointed Chairman for our local area, and I went to a Cambridge area meeting with other solicitors for a section of East Anglia. We met at various hotels in Huntingdon, Cambridge and even Newmarket racecourse. It was an excellent idea and allowed solicitors from all over the area to talk to each other and compare our duty solicitor police stations and court. It was at a cost. We were paid £100 each and given out travelling costs.

13. Terrifying Judges

I think the most terrifying encounters I have had with judges is not in court conducting defence and cross-examining prosecution witnesses but appearing before a Taxing Master in the High Court and an experienced Taxing Registrar in a big county court.

When your case was finished, you would send your bill to the court to be *taxed on as provisional basis*. The bill was very detailed and had to be set out with special numerous columns and sometimes there were pages and pages of it. It was an expertise to draft these bills which were usually done by a costs draftsman whose firms seemed to be squirrelled away in a back street of London.

In my Gillick case, the 10 pages of the bill set out on A3 paper were sent into Court, the High Court in the Strand in London; it was in 2 parts. A column of costs that had to be paid by the opposite party, and a column of costs that I could claim from the legal aid fund, not payable by the losing party.

It soon came back in the post with various red pen marks scribbled all over it on every page and signed at the end by **Master Prince**. They were the costs that the master disallowed and he'd even struck through some fees of the barrister we had used and he was a Queen's Counsel too.

What was I to do? I thought all enormous fees exhorted by Queen's Counsel were excessive, but I couldn't argue that—against my own barrister. And I mean he had struck out great wads of money—£500 here, £750 there.

So I asked for an appointment to review the taxation but the barrister would have come with me to argue his own case to justify his own fees. I had no idea why £3,000 was a fair sum or not for one day of a hearing in the Court of Appeal. My salary was only £8,000 for the whole year.

So, the Queen's Counsel came down from his chambers in Liverpool and we both waited in a corridor in the High Court. It was just like waiting for ***Jarndyce and Jarndyce in Dickens' Bleak House.*** The corridor was dark and forbidding. The seat was a hard bench and silent barristers strode past in twos with gowns flowing. We waited, as if outside the Headmaster's study.

The High Court

The door beside us had a notice on white card pushed in the brass holder, announcing this was Master Prince's room.

We heard a sound from the other side of the oak door—"Come!"—it seemed to be an order rather than a request.

I looked at the Q.C. anxiously. It was up to him if he wanted to get his money back.

"Yes Mr Clarke, sit down," another order. "And who is that with you?"

"Mr X, the Q.C. in the case."

I saw a slight raising of the eyebrows. Maybe he wondered why this country bumpkin couldn't argue for the costs himself. He didn't know that this country bumpkin had never been before a Taxing Master in his life and was on the point of running away or busting into tears.

And so it went on. The barrister did argue for his costs, and it shocked me how arbitrary it all was.

"Why do you think your fee of £3,000 is worth it?" the Master asked.

I looked to the QC. He said it was an important case, involved lots of research... blah... blah... Sounded good but unconvincing. Maybe I could have said that myself.

"OK," the master said. "I'll allow you £2,800."

And that was that. It was like an auction. Maybe the Master was testing us and made us come all this way to see if we were serious about our arguments.

On another case, I had to appear before a Taxing Registrar in Bristol County court. In this case, the costs to be taxed were those to be paid by the opposition so I had an opponent sitting there glaring at me on the other side of the table. And he also seemed to know what he was doing.

Well, I waited for the onslaught but it would be more difficult than appearing before the Master in the High Court. I had an opponent who would like to avoid paying any costs even though he lost the case. So the Registrar proceeded:

"Well, Mr Clarke, page 5—how do you justify £60 for reading the medical record?"

"I did spend 3 hours."

"3 hours?" chirped up the opponent. "It's quite straightforward; probably 1 and a half hours are sufficient."

I thought quickly. I did take 3 hours to read it; surely, I should get what I did. But maybe these two were more experienced than me. Maybe they would take 1 and half hours.

Then I realised none of us had time to argue. It was like an auction as I remembered from the Gillick taxation some years before.

"Sir, I'll take 2 hours."

"Right," commented the Register, "next item—page 6."

After another 20 minutes, it was finished, and I walked out into this strange town I'd never been to before. It was the nicest sight I beheld for a long time.

Leaving aside whether judges frighten me or not, my theory is that those who intimidate you usually need to do so to bolster their position or authority. However the higher up the hierarchy, the less likely judges need to be intimidating.

When you appeal against a sentence imposed in the Crown Court, you can appeal to the Court of Appeal (Criminal Division) which usually consists of 2 judges but they are far more intelligent than the Crown Court judges, and usually come from Oxbridge colleges and have a quick grasp of the issues.

In Criminal law, I only had experience of the Court of Appeal on one occasion. My client was appealing against a sentence of 6 years. The law is that on appeal you must prove that the sentence was **manifestly excessive.** You must also ask for permission to appeal from a single judge.

Well, I sat at the back of the court waiting for my case to come up. When it did, I was expecting arguments to be heard from both sides. Remember the Grounds of Appeal plus case law had been lodged in writing already.

The leading judge addressed the prosecution:

"We have read the papers and have considered that the appropriate figure is 7 years."

Before I could think about anything, the prosecution replied, "Yes."

And that was it. No arguments. it was all done in about 10 seconds. Of course, if the prosecution thought they had a chance to disagree, I suppose they would have said so but they didn't and then the next case was called.

I was very impressed.

14. Two Famous Judges

I went to a small school of about 60 boys in the 1950s in Southwold Suffolk. One of my friends was a boy called Charles Backie. We were both 10/13 at the time.

60 year later, I met him again but this time at my house in Cambridgeshire; he and his parents had emigrated to New Zealand, and he was coming back to England to visit Suffolk and his old school.

However, he had become a Crown Court Judge in New Zealand and he recounted to me the most peculiar case he had to judge. He had become the Chief Judge of the Pitcairn islands over which New Zealand had territorial jurisdiction. The islands were very remote and promiscuity among men living there was tolerated which in other countries would be considered as child abuse.

In 1999, a police officer visited the island. One girl aged 15 wanted to press rape charges. Eventually, a trial ensued before Chief Justice Blackie, and he sentenced those found guilty of such offences. The case created a great deal of bitterness. 6 convicted men lodged an appeal against their conviction; it was refused, and they therefore appealed to the Privy Council in London. Their appeals were dismissed.

Later, Charles Blackie (illustrated below) came to see me in 2016 and stayed with me and my wife and gave his account of what happened in the trial 17 years before.

Who was the other famous Judge? My father. I have written about his fame in a previous book, but it only came home to me how he was revered when he died. The major newspapers included a large obituary in 1989. Then there was his memorial service after his death and cremation. But I went to the memorial service in Lincoln's Inn chapel which was full to overflowing and there was Lord Hailsham, a former Lord Chancellor, who gave a speech about his life.

I felt quite humble because I never really respected him and his job when he was around, and I thought that he disapproved of my marriage to my wife, which coloured my judgement. Well, I can't undo my attitude to him at the time he was alive but the respect people exhibited to him after he died made me think twice about my attitude to him.

15. Magistrates

The absolute backbone of the legal system in England is the Magistrates Court System. However, ironically, most magistrates courts are empty except for those participating in cases or watching them because they have an interest.

It may be a stupid observation but people pack sports stadiums around in England, they go to plays and other entertainment but people don't go and watch cases unless they are law students or have a specific interest.

We hear and follow important cases in the higher courts, the latest as I write is the Wagatha case in the higher civil court and a film has been made of it. Drama documentaries have been made of cases but it's happening every day in the high streets of England.

And the stars of these 'plays' or 'dramas' are the magistrates who can send people to prison, make judgements on people's actions or acquit people. They can be the sword against arbitrary prosecutions.

So though I am a mild lawyer who is not an activist, I do believe in the system and how fair it can be. Who are these magistrates? I saw them every day, chatted to them and joked with them but I did feel I should not get too matey with them.

I didn't have any of them as a close friend. They didn't say things like the following, which they could have done:

- "What you said was rubbish, did you really think you could convince us of them?"
- "How can you act for that crook; you should know he was guilty."
- "He is laughing at you; he is using you."
- "He knows he's guilty."
- "We were laughing at your suggestion put to us."

So, my feeling is that we backed off each other and kept our distance to preserve our independence.

One magistrate comes to mind. I forget his name, but he liked to be original. He talked slowly and in a measured tone, which somehow sounded threatening. I think he was a teacher at his local secondary school. In fact, when I had my smallholding, I bought a trailer off him but apart from chatting about the trailer, we didn't chat about my work.

If someone had to pay a fine or that was on the cards, he might ask him or her, "How much money do you have in your pocket?"

Sometimes the client had quite a bit and so he would be fined that amount. I'm not sure if that 'means test' was legal but he said it nevertheless and seemed to set him apart from the other magistrates.

I never knew why they wanted to be a magistrate. Powerful men in a locality in history might be magistrates as a matter of course; they are mentioned in novels to highlight their position in the narrative.

They obviously have power, but they are not paid except for their expenses. They are recommended by local bodies, by trade unions and the like.

I'll just end this narrative with a short story or event in my local court. A man came into the back of the court and brought his dog tied to a bit of string. We noticed him but tried to take no notice, thinking he had made a mistake.

But he still stood there. The magistrates are in charge of their own court and order and discipline there. The magistrates I have mentioned above pointed out publicly that he should take his dog out because they are not allowed.

He didn't move and tension heightened. Was he making a point or what? The magistrates repeated the request which had become an order. He didn't move. The magistrates asked the local policeman to escort him out; there was a scuffle, almost a fight and he was arrested and hustled out.

Later, he appeared in the dock on a charge but before different magistrates.

16. Going to Court and the Smallholding

After being qualified, my wife and I suddenly decided to go self-sufficient and buy a smallholding. Looking back, it's difficult to imagine why we did that but there are lots of things we do in our past that we later wonder why we did it.

Anyhow, the point is we bought a 5-acre smallholding. But I decided not to give up the job of being a solicitor and I never did.

The two occupations sometimes got a bit mixed up but no matter. I had pigs and sold the fat pigs after they had been butchered. The Abattoir would split the carcass in half, and I'd put one half in the passenger side of my 3-wheel Reliant car I had at the time (but that spawns another group of stories I won't recount here).

I had to collect the half carcass at lunchtime. I whipped off at one o'clock while the court was not sitting, grabbed the carcass and put it in the car and then went back to Court. I had parked opposite the Magistrate's court for quick access; then I went in the Court and finished whatever business I had there.

I came out with the client chatting away about his case, saying it was lucky he just got probation. He smiled as he walked and then stared at a car parked there; it was my car but he didn't know that. For status reasons, I didn't tell all and sundry I had a 3-wheel Reliant.

But he wasn't staring at the car as such. I pretended not to notice his distraction and carried on talking; but he was staring at the pig carcass whose head was lounging against the back of the seat with one eye watching my client.

I hurried on, hustling him into the office. He never told me what he had been staring at and I didn't mention what car I had.

On another occasion, the Reliant broke down at the office, as it did quite often. My conveyancing clerk was very amenable and said he'd tow me back home after the office closed. I got in the Reliant and he got into his posh car. We got to the next town where there was a big roundabout opposite the local police station I appeared in constantly.

However, it was difficult steering a 3-wheel car while being towed and I wasn't concentrating. Suddenly, the rope snapped, on the roundabout opposite the police station… We mended the rope and I got the car home. No one noticed the breakdown and the fact that the local posh solicitor owned a Reliant.

It was harder to combine appearing at court on time and dealing with the smallholding before dawn. If I had to take the sheep or pigs to the abattoir, I'd have to get up early, load the animals and take them 6 miles away to the abattoir. I didn't wear my suit or wash before I went.

Even worse was going to the market to sell live animals at the auction. That was 40 miles away and would take me, at 40 miles an hour, about an hour, and up and out of bed at 4 am.

But then I had to get back, put the trailer away, wash and dress and get to Court for 9.30. There was the client waiting, trying to appear patient.

"Well, I'm here early but only just got here: where have you been—just got out of bed?" he added to press his point home. He continued, "I don't get up this early, but I have to, don't I, or a warrant would be issued for my arrest!" He looked at me as if waiting for a word of praise.

I mumbled in reply as I got papers out of my briefcase.

17. Countryside Crime

Most crime by far is committed in the town and urban areas. There are more people there, more things to be pinched, more people squashed together causing stress and assaults.

But the pure emptiness of the countryside creates crime because of its emptiness of people, which means no one can see you and there is no light about to illuminate the crime.

The greatest number of victims in the desolate countryside are farmers and landowners. When I ran a smallholding, as well as being a solicitor, I went away on holiday and when I came back, two of my metal gates had disappeared; yes, a whole metal gate 8 foot long and 600 yards from the nearest tarmac road and just *'walked'* across a grass field.

So it wasn't a quick in and out and disappear down a dark alley job, with the stolen items tucked inside a jacket pocket.

No -it was a job totally in the dark and necessitating tramping across a grass field in the dark; you might trip over a dip in the lie of the land. How did you know that in the dark you were tramping to where there might be a gate to steal?

Well, you have time in the countryside to think about your crime. All you need is a torch and, oh yes, for an 8-foot gate, you needed help to carry the thing, for in winter you'd get stuck on the wet grass even if you knew where you are aiming for. In any event, on this occasion, there were no vehicle track marks.

Talking about farmers, I was told it was important to put your postcode on any machine likely to be stolen. My ride-on mower in the dark got pinched and I made a claim from the insurance; on the new mower I scratched my postcode; a few years later, I moved to a place 400 miles away—with a different postcode!

Back to the gates, I now know why they are hung on hangers one upside-down; so you couldn't unhook the gate and walk off with it. Never did so many gates on a smallholding have chains and padlocks hung around them and their adjoining hanging post.

Having rubbish dumped on your land or even in the access to your land is another crime suffered in the countryside where it is dark. I had over 100 worn tyres dropped in the ditch adjoining my land. That is a crime and if they are dropped just on your land or in a ditch owned by the adjoining farmer, the farmer will have to pay for it to be taken away.

On a bigger scale, whole machines are taken from farmyards meaning their security is almost impossible to implement; that causes great distress to isolated farmers; no wonder the suicide rate of farmers is one of the highest in the land.

Sometime ago, when I lived on a smallholding near my land, some caravans parked up and looked as if they were going to settle there for good on a grass track called a *'Drove'* in the fens area.

The police came but could do nothing unless a crime had been committed. They visited the caravan dwellers, but they knew they could not be moved. Eventually, a lateral-thinking policeman realised that the caravan owners needed water and they were taking it not from a stream but from a cattle trough owned by the local farmer.

That was theft though it might be difficult to mount a prosecution... of water. However, the owners were reminded by the uniformed boys in blue and the caravans had gone by the next morning.

In my practice, I came across a more serious type of crime, hare coursing. Criminals would travel up from the towns nearer London in their 4-wheel-drive vehicles with their greyhound dogs. They would go to areas they knew had hares and the chase would be lit up with the headlights of their expensive Land Rovers.

Most of this hare coursing happened in Lincolnshire because of its flat rural countryside. However, everything changed in 2022 when the law was changed.

Before, you had to catch them trespassing doing the hare coursing. However, when the law was changed, it was a crime going equipped with the intent to trespass with a dog to do hare coursing.

It always involved criminal gangs from outside the county. They were usually involved in a whole range of criminality other than hare coursing, including possession of firearms.

In December 2022, there were 527 such crimes intimidating local farmers. The Lincolnshire police invested in a rural team. With the new law, the criminal can have their cars and dogs seized as well as mobile phones. They can also be ordered to pay for the looking after the seized dogs by the police.

This changed the whole attitude to the police by the local community. They could see police on the ground, and they got positive feedback because they could see technology being used. It was an abhorrent crime from a cruelty point of view, but if they were caught there was one tool in the armoury of the law which helped as the new law allowed.

Once caught and arrested, they were taken to the local police station in police cars and questioned. They were then released on bail hundreds of miles from their homes in Essex. My client asked me, "Where is my Land Rover?"

"It's been seized," I replied and shrugged.

"How do I get home?" he asked, looking disbelieving and a bit desperate.

"I don't know," I replied honestly and then added, trying to be helpful, "There is a train station over there, but I have no idea of the times on Sunday afternoon. If you are going down south, you'll certainly have to change at Cambridge; ask at the station. Anyway, I'm glad you got bail. I'll write to you."

And I slumped into my car and wended my way home.

18. Prison Law

Having slated the probation service in the previous chapter, I will now shine a light on the lawyers acting for prisoners.

When I first did Prison Law, I soon discovered there was an Association of Prisoner Lawyers who seemed regularly to contact each other through the internet. You could just ask a question on something you were dealing with and then send it out into the ether and it would reach all the other lawyers. Some of the questions or comments I set out:

"Watch judge so and so; I've just appeared before him; he doesn't like women solicitors."

"Remember the new case concerning Parole. It's just been published called X vs Y."

"Can anyone cover my case as an agent at Wayland tomorrow; my barrister is booked for something else?"

There were favourite barristers who were very good at advising on prison law and they could get an advice to you quickly. They also ran courses in their chambers and then you would meet all the solicitors that you knew through the emails that had gone back and forth. An excellent network and I must say that I miss that fraternity.

One barrister was called Kris Gledhill; Doughty Street chambers were probably the best chambers for Prison law and associated subjects and is a few doors from Charles Dickens house in the same street—very appropriate.

All very far from 1972 when Lord Denning (illustrated above), an otherwise liberal judge, did not consider that prisoners had any rights that could be protected. Doughty Street chambers 50 years later is choc-a-bloc with KCs, the majority of whom practise Prison Law.

19. Prisons and Farm Animals

When I was a prosecuting solicitor, Whitemoor prison was built in the 1990s. I had a smallholding, and it came to my notice that several prisons had farms adjoining them and with animals. I think they were set up some years ago as a therapeutic environment for trusted prisoners to work in.

At Littlehey prison (illustrated above) near Huntingdon, they had a farm and pigs. I rang the farm and wanted some Large Black piglets they had for sale. I drove my car and trailer there, had a chat with the farm manager and bought some piglets.

As I drove out, I glanced to one side and saw Littlehey prison itself, a prison reserved for sex offenders. I knew nothing about it and it wasn't a remand prison. None of my clients I represented in court would come here while they were waiting for their trial.

After court, once my clients had been sent to prison, my job was over; I had not yet been introduced to Prison Law.

Another prison the other side of East Anglia, an open prison, had a farm which dealt with heavy carthorses, Suffolk's. The prisoners who were trusted, and most were because it was an open prison, dealt with the farm.

I never had dealings with this farm as I had no carthorses but both those prisons were an excellent therapeutic idea for prisoners. You don't argue with animals, and they respond with affection if they are treated well. Animals hold no grudges. Prisoners usually are sentenced because of criminality in the form of antisocial behaviour against other humans.

Unfortunately, while I acted for prisoners as a solicitor, both these farms lost their connections with their adjoining prisons; it was a false way to save money. What a pity.

20. Prisoners and Pleading for Them

Of course, I had dealt with prisoners as soon as I was qualified to appear in court, but I didn't go down to the cells very often because my first cases involved people on bail.

However, I soon got a shock with my first serious client who might go to prison. I mitigated and tried to persuade the magistrates to give him one more chance. I didn't believe my own speech but after they retired, I soon realised what was going to happen.

Initially, before the docks were surrounded with bulletproof glass, the defendant would either sit in the dock or even stand beside me, all very civilised. Then, while the magistrates were out, two policemen would walk into the court and stand at the back. The magistrates had sent a message out that they were going to send him to prison.

Alternatively, he would be standing in the dock.

Simple as I was in my early days, I somehow thought they might let him go home to pack or go to a private room to say goodbye to his loved ones. NO! When the magistrates came back into the court, they ended the sentencing remarks with the words: "…so you will be given a term of 4 months."

And then, I learnt to hold my breath. Was he going to have a suspended sentence? If so, the sentence would continue with the words, "…which term will be suspended for 2 years."

And you could hear a sigh of relief from the client and the relatives. He had got off yet again.

Indeed, I have acted for a client who got a suspended sentence and a few months later came back to court for the very same offence yet again. My mitigation was more desperate:

"His wife /partner is devastated."

"He so regrets what he has done."

"He just can't believe what a fool he has been."

"Yes, he deserves to go to prison."

Or even, "He wants to go to prison but I feel he cannot see the mitigation I am now going to put forward."

I tried to sound sincere and genuine and used phrases from the Thesaurus in my mind. There was only one client whom I didn't say all this for. He had just been released from prison, but he had been caught on the way home burgling a solicitor's office. He couldn't cope with being in the community. In his case, he wanted to go back inside. It was nice and safe in prison. Everything was done for you. So, I said, and it was difficult to do, "He wants to go back inside; he should go back inside…"

The problem with that mitigation is that only a nutter wants to go back to prison, and the court adjourned his case for reports including investigating his mental health.

I'm not sure if he got bail in the meantime. A difficult decision for the magistrates.

Fast forward some 20 years when I was really experienced in Prisoners and Prison Law. I acted for serious offenders who had been convicted and were undertaking long sentences. I still did mitigation for them, in Parole cases before a Parole panel. However, that bench was more sophisticated, but it was still the question of risk. In layman's terms, the question was: Is he likely to do it again?

However, before the magistrates, the question is: Should he be forgiven, should he be given a second chance?

Before the Parole board, it is: Is he still a danger to the public (after all the courses he has done inside)?

It's still all about advocacy and persuading the persons listening that what you're saying has a ring of truth.

21. Shocking Videos

When I first practised, we didn't have videos, nor would I know what a video was. We had forensic photographs of dead bodies and knives with a calibration beside them but that was all in the photographic field of evidence.

Then street cameras appeared. Indeed, there was no guidance how to use them in court nor how to use stills taken from them but technology advances.

My first viewing of a video was in the police station, for the best evidence of what happened in a fight late at night was the nearest street camera. For the first time, I saw violence though I'd never been in a fight myself, and it was shocking.

I distinctly viewed one fight in the street under a lamp light. The scene seemed to be outside a pub. The aggressor stepped forward and head-butted the victim. He dropped on the pavement and lay still had I just seen a murder? —and I turned to the officer with an unfeigned look of surprise but immediately made my face plain. I didn't want to show shock. They might think I was wet behind the ears.

If the truth were known, in my day I doubt if any solicitor had been involved or seen any fight. If they were not in the police station, they might be at home listening to Brahms or Beethoven.

But after viewing a few videos, you had to be alert as to what you saw. I had to remember that the people in whose hands the fate of my client rested were the Magistrates or a Jury.

If a figure was running down the street, the police might say, ***"There is your client running down the street!"***

And the policeman wanted to carry on quickly. But I intervened, "I don't think so."

We could argue on the question of identification during the interview but if at least some of the jury couldn't identify who was running down the street, I had raised the issue, there and then.

On another case, there was or seemed to be a riot in the street late at night with 15 to 20 kids running, no, chasing a victim and then laying into him. It was important to identify my client once again; he might not be the aggressor; he may be there or not or may look like one of the others. He may not have kicked the victim. Trying to see what he did may make the difference between prison or not, guilt or innocence. The police were not the decision makers. The jury was.

But of course, it worked both ways. The 'know-alls' and 'streetwise juveniles' would swear blind they hadn't done this or that. I nodded sagely, considering his denials. The more he denied, the deeper the trench he was digging. I noted it all down in my notebook.

The police had told me he was seen in the shop which had been shoplifted, but my client denied anyone was in there; but then the police, after giving me initial disclosure, suddenly announced they had been given a video from the shop. They said they hadn't seen it but we all might as well see it together.

I was a bit worried about that but my client hadn't twigged that he might be falling into a trap. After all, it might show he wasn't there and he would be released. The police didn't offer to show it to me first. The police went through the formalities of an interview and then asked the client to give his account. So off he went saying he was elsewhere, never been in the shop. I wrote notes.

Then the police officer shrugged and said, "Well, let's see what the video shows. Certainly, you might not be there."

So he slowly put the disc into the machine and it was played. We saw the client in the shop, saw the client clearly walk around suspiciously, walk to one of the cabinets and then put a package in his inside pocket and walk out. I asked the police to stop the tape as I thought my client wanted to have a word with me.

22. First Cases at Brighton

I think my first defended case as I can remember was acting for an old lady who was in her car at some lights which were red. They went green and her car slid backwards and hit the car behind.

She was adamant that as the car was behind her, he must have gone forward and hit her. She was a strong-willed lady and was sure that might have happened, so she pleaded not guilty to a charge of careless driving.

She was not a good witness because she was so assertive but because of her age, it was clear to the magistrates she might have made a mistake and on setting off she might have put the car in reverse.

The trouble was she was convicted of careless driving but worse than that, she was ordered to take a driving test again.

She was mortified and I think gave up driving. Maybe it's a warning to me as I am now her age of 77.

The firm I joined in Brighton was my first job doing just litigation. After a few days, the partner approached me and asked me to carry on a case that the clerk who I replaced had started. He handed me the file and it seemed rather thin. I looked inside. It was almost empty, but I found a statement and it seemed to be about a driver who had hit an American tourist in Brighton. So the American was the Plaintiff who I was acting for? The date of the accident was written on the front of the file, 2 and a half years ago! I spoke to the secretary and asked if a claim had been issued in the County Court; she didn't think so but if it was, the plaint fee would have been paid. It hadn't. I was then reminded by the partner that there was a limitation period of 3 years to issue a claim.

This was bad. What was I to do? Well, the secretary admitted the file had been lost. The only thing I could do was to write to the other side and ask for copies of our correspondence with them. If they delayed, they could have let the case go beyond the 3-year limitation period. I would have to start again damn quick.

I had the client in, admitted what we had done or not done and took a statement from him. I wrote to the hospital he had attended and got copies of the medical report. I forget what happened, but the case was settled, and I issued a claim in time and caught up.

But that sort of situation is not good for the nerves when you have just qualified as a solicitor.

In one case, I saw another old lady who had been arrested for shoplifting. She had been sent out to me as the duty solicitor at Court for the day for advice because she entered an equivocal plea. She was unrepresented and pleaded guilty but when asked for mitigation, she said she didn't mean to steal.

The clerk advised her to see the duty solicitor.

I asked her what she wanted to do. She said she wanted it over and completed that day. She said her husband didn't know about it but would if she had a trial; what was she to do?

I told her to go in and plead guilty as she had before. I would not mitigate on her behalf as I might be compromising my duty to the court of misleading it. I told her when she was asked to say she was sorry she did it and that was all. She had no previous convictions, and I was sure she could get a fine or even a conditional discharge.

The point is from her point of view she wanted it over and done with quickly and without any fuss which might otherwise attract the attention of the press and so her husband might know.

I wonder if much later she did tell her husband.

23. Left-Wing Attitudes

When I started work in Brighton, I was full of the keenness of righting wrongs, helping poor people and generally being left-wing as I could though if you asked me, I wouldn't be aware of that attitude at the time. It was just so obvious.

I subscribed to all the pamphlets issued by the then Department of Health and Social Security. Pamphlets on Unemployment Benefit, Supplementary Benefits and Housing Benefits. I knew them very well and kept them in an alphabetical file.

I went down to the Citizens Advice Bureau and volunteered to give free legal advice in evening sessions once a week. Poor people came in, people who couldn't help themselves and I had such ardour and keenness that I almost put off the clients who just wanted quite mild and minimal advice. Brighton was quite an alternative place and the manager of the CAB took on board such keenness that would serve her purpose being herself also a left-wing activist.

Then I came across a charity called New Bridge who helped prisoners by sending volunteers to visit them; I signed up for this and indeed, when my mother sent me £400 as a one-off present, with a flourish I gave it all to New Bridge.

Both and my wife started visiting Ford Open Prison (illustrated above) and befriending prisoners there. One was about to be released and I gave him our address and invited him to stay with us. I felt very worthy (and naïve about that invitation).

The chap came, we gave him a meal and bedded him down on our sofa. The next day, I sat up and stretched feeling all's right with the world and wondered if our ex-prisoner had finished with the bathroom. The door was open, so I thought I'd go downstairs. Maybe he wants some breakfast. He'd not know where all the utensils are. I walked into the sitting room and glanced around. He was nowhere to be seen; the sheets, blankets, in fact, everything else had gone except the sofa.

My first learning experience started slowly to dent my liberal adopted nature and as time went on practising litigation, my liberality slowly deflated.

24. Cases Under New Case Law. New Aggravating and Mitigating Features

In criminal law, more than civil law, from time to time new laws were passed. We went on courses and had to learn them, especially when we might have a client who was to be charged under the new law. But it didn't happen straight away; obviously there was discussion in Parliament, our legal magazines set out what was to be proposed and then we went on courses.

It was the prosecution/ the police that had to tackle new laws first in practice, in Criminal Law at least.

Jumping now to ***Aggravating*** features; all criminal offences had *aggravating* features and mitigating features. There was a maximum and minimum sentencing guideline, but *aggravating* features might make the sentence higher up the scale. Drunkenness was an *aggravating* feature, of course; i.e., the sentence you might be given would be higher if it was committed when you were drunk.

You had one-third off if you pleaded guilty.

I only had one case I can remember where a new aggravating feature was added either as a new law or as an amended sentencing guideline.

Racially aggravated offences attracted a higher than usual sentence. The problem was how to interpret the facts of the case to the term ***racial.***

My client was in the pub having a drink with a black guy. They were friends but he was getting more and more drunk. I should say that he was not aggressive at all to his friend because he was black but as they argued on issues, the conversation became more heated about Nelson Mandela and the black segregation in South Africa. As I can remember, my client sincerely believed that Mandela was wrong; we didn't go into the detail of each and every point in the argument.

However, my client got more and more heated mainly because he was drunk, though I think he believed in his argument, and he suddenly got up and head-butted the friend and a fight started. The police came, and he was arrested for common assault. OK. He was drunk which was an aggravating feature to the common assault charge (he pleaded guilty).

However, he was charged with **racially** aggravated common assault. That meant he could get a higher sentence because of the **racial aggravation**. I had to think about that. Certainly, the argument was, I suppose, a racial argument, but did that mean that the sentence should be higher because of his views or was his assault against his friend just because he was black? Certainly not.

Well, he pleaded guilty.

What should the court do about the sentence if he didn't agree as to the **racial aggravation** bit? However, if the magistrates consider that there was racial aggravation and it would influence them in sentencing, there could be a trial on that point.

However, they did sentence him and did think that the aggravation was racial, BUT decided they would give him the same sentence in any event. He didn't want to appeal the sentence he got, on the grounds that the magistrates decided the attack was racially aggravated.

Of course, in all cases of appeal, the Crown Court can increase the sentence on appeal as well as lower it and he didn't want to attract more light on the racial aspect of the case which might even head him to a prison sentence. When this case was dealt with some time ago, racial issues were not as important as they are now.

25. Clever Crooks

Crooks are never clever. As I have said before, there are easier ways of making money over the long term. Of course, that might have changed now with the internet and scams; but in my day crooks or criminals were mostly thieves, burglars and the like.

One class, if you can call it that, were gypsies. There was a prejudice against them in the area where I practised. If there was a crime, the word went about that it was probably the gypsies. I will not comment on that prejudice. The ones I acted for took pride in not living off the state but dealt with in cash for the most part.

However, the ones I did deal with who clashed with the police were very easy to get on with. They were usually loyal to one solicitor.

On one occasion, they were quite clever if you can call it that. They used to live on caravan sites which the police for the most part didn't want to go too near. But on one occasion, they must have had a tip-off about drugs. If you walked onto a site, you might be met with a few dogs barking at you. caravans in a row, washing out and so on. Nothing to raise your suspicions.

However, a tip-off means there was something irregular.

When I went to the police station, the police disclosed to me what they had found in the middle of the central track of the caravan site, a small trapdoor, covered with dirt. Nothing that you might look at twice. However, if you cleared away the dirt, there emerged a sort of metal cover rather like a drain cover.

On lifting the cover, the police found a huge shipping container with masses of drugs hidden down there. So the culprits must had dug a huge hole with a digger, inserted a shipping container and then covered it over with the excavated dirt.

What an immense project. The culprits must have relied very much on the loyalty of those on the caravan site who would not tell; however, someone did.

Of course, I no longer have the file now so I don't know why he pleaded guilty or whether he had a trial, and why he was suspected more than others. I just give this as an unusual example of some of my more colourful criminal escapades—which was unsuccessful.

In another case, once again involving my client who was a gypsy, he and his friend saw an all-terrain vehicle (ATV) parked to the side of a house. He went to the next-door neighbour and said he wanted to see the person in that house.

The neighbour innocently said he won't be able to see him as he had gone away. Whereupon my client and his friend silently and quickly wired up the ATV and drove it away.

So, no balaclavas on, no motorbike helmets on, no looking clandestine; just an apparent innocent question to a rather gullible neighbour. However, the client and his brother were not too bright because they used this method of stealing quite often. The police looked up that type of crime, identified my client because of his previous modus operandi, swooped on the caravan park where he lived and there behind his caravan was the ATV. He hadn't had time to sell it on.

Finally, I am loath to refer to some client's nationality but when Romania joined the European Union, I had a few clients of that nationality who were quite clever. That may or may not have been because of their nationality, I shall never know.

One put a strip of two-sided Sellotape in the exit slit where cash came out of an ATM usually situated outside or in the wall of a petrol station. A person would approach the ATM to get cash. He or she put in the card, requested cash of say £50 and pushed the button. No cash came out. They waited and waited and then shrugged their shoulders, and either went into the petrol station to complain or went back to their car. My client, who had been watching, immediately walked up to the to the ATM, put some tweezers into the cash opening and pulled out the cash which had stuck onto the Sellotape. Of course, a camera saw him, he was identified and arrested. I don't applaud this, but it did show a sort of devious cleverness.

26. A Sad Case That Might Not Have Been a Crime

Am I speaking in riddles when I say this chapter is about sad cases that might not be crimes? Whatever is this two-faced lawyer talking about, in riddles!

Well, not quite but I entitled it and I did to attract your attention. The riddle is, what crime is not a crime if it is carried out successfully?

Well, that is sort of what I mean though I'm sure there could be some clever barrister or even a KC who could argue with me and say my riddle is nonsense, so I'll carry on with the facts.

I had a client who had a girlfriend, and they were very much in love. However, they had a problem which weighed heavily upon them both. He had a child from a former relationship, but he had been refused access to the child. I forget for what reason or why it might have been justified. Suffice it to say, my client could see no way out of this impasse and it got them both depressed.

Eventually one evening they made an agreement, a joint suicide pact. They would kill each other and that would be the end of their joint problems. They knew it was going to be difficult and they may not have the courage to carry it out so they had a drinking spree together in their room where they lived, emptying a big bottle of whiskey.

They were just about done with it but almost incapable when they undressed their tops and he marked a spot on his partner's chest where he was to strike her and she did the same on his head. He went out in the shed adjoining the house and got an axe, for this was the implement to do the killing. (Incidentally, he must have been incapably drunk to think of an axe; but I think by this stage they hadn't agreed how they were going to kill each other.)

They were dead drunk by this time and there on the floor was an empty bottle of whiskey. She was more incapable than him, just about. They had never got around to an agreement as to who would act first. He whereupon got the axe and struck her on the head and killed her. Then he says he felt drowsy and became insensible.

Someone called the police, maybe because of some suspicion; they broke in and found him. He was arrested for Murder. He came into my hands and in Court he pleaded not guilty but guilty to Manslaughter on the grounds of Diminished Responsibility. I must say I had my doubts about that defence because usually, using drink as a defence is not permissible.

However, the CPS considered my client's plea and accepted it as did the court. He was given 4 years for Manslaughter.

Now my riddle is this. If somehow, he planned to help her commit suicide, that is a crime. It's difficult to image but if they both killed each other, both would be dead so there would be no one to prosecute. In any event, it is not a crime to commit suicide or try to do so.

Maybe all that is an academic exercise. How can you kill someone with an axe and then kill yourself with the same implement?

I think I'll back off the story now.

27. Stand-Off on Mother's Day

One case I had, had very exciting facts almost like an old-style gangster type case but that was rare, and I never had the same type again in all my 44 years. My client had planned to rob a flower shop just on or after Mother's Day because he knew that their tills would be full of money.

He was a hardened criminal and indeed he had just come out of prison having been given a 12-year sentence for armed robbery. He hadn't learnt from this sentence and had decided to take a firearm. However, the police had had a tip-off about the robbery both as to the time and place and did a stakeout of the place. They watched and saw him draw up at the place, go inside and a few moments later come out.

Suddenly, the police came out of hiding and a couple of the gang was caught. My client however ran off and started across a nearby field. A senior police officer chased him and they got near to each other. The officer was carrying a revolver. Suddenly, according to the evidence given in court later, my client turned and he had a gun in his hand. The officer had one in his hand, and they faced each other.

The officer said quite carefully in the Crown Court that it seemed an age as they faced each other, no one dropped their guns for a second or two then my client did; he was captured, handcuffed and taken off.

At the Crown Court, he pleaded guilty to armed robbery and associated charges and went back to prison for another 12 years. He obviously didn't learn but it was not of the norm for the countryside where I practised, a countryside growing lots of flowers ready for Mother's Day.

28. Fraternisation Between Barristers, Judges and Solicitors

A lot of my friends who are not in the law can't quite get their head around how we lawyers all fraternise with each other but at the same time, there is a manufactured gap between Plaintiff and Defendant or Prosecution and Defence in Court; but then there they are all together in the robing room at court, friends with each other, and calling each other by their first names.

Indeed, the wording on documents and in court implies that your *opposite party* is not your friend. They are your 'opponent', 'the opposition'. But it has been going on for centuries: how can that work?

There is no other sphere in society where this happens. No doctor opposes another even in war—they all have the same one aim and that happens in other professions, except of course in sport where you do have an opponent. Maybe a court scenario is like a sport but I dare not say that really as it would diminish the seriousness of court cases.

Well, the court system is a 'manufactured' competition. You call in court your opponent 'your friend' or if he or she is a barrister, 'my learned friend'.

The advocates are from the word go disarmed from being aggressive to each other.

There is the Bar Association and the Inns of Court where they fraternise together. There is a Law Society and Local Law Societies for solicitors where they all get together.

In my period of practising, there was a sort of social gap between barristers and solicitors but there was a bigger social gap between some type of clients and their lawyers. That may not be so as much today as I think lawyers feel much more for their clients and their causes; that is partly I think because social class barriers have slowly dissolved and in law at least Human Rights have arisen.

Of course, there is no 'cause' for a criminal but there is the protection of the law which your opponent respects.

However, as I write, there are certain 'causes' within the criminal law where, for instance, a defendant causes criminal damage to support his or her cause. The toppling of the Colston statue into the tidal basin at Bristol, with the defence of doing it with reasonable excuse. As a defendant, you would prefer to have a barrister or solicitor who believes in your cause. Obviously so in Northern Ireland and terrorist cases.

In that case, you would as a client pick your barrister carefully; one who supports your cause. In my Gillick case, because she felt so strongly about her case, I asked her to choose her barrister. She chose a QC who was a Catholic. I didn't think he was exceptional, but it helped a great deal having a barrister communicating with such an intense client.

What of judges? How can you be clubbish with a judge who judges your case and your advocacy when in the past that judge was a mere barrister and before that a junior barrister appearing before senior judges.

I was brought up in a hybrid situation. I was not a lawyer and lived with my father, a Judge. I obviously fraternised with him as my father but also saw him in Court being stern with advocates. I then had lunch accompanying him at Lincoln's Inn with very senior judges, indeed top judges whose judgements I studied at University at the time. I can't explain what I thought at the time in my early 20s with long hair, speaking to Lord Denning, one of my father's greatest friends, and Lord Hailsham, the Lord Chancellor of the time and who gave a speech at my father's memorial service after he died.

Whatever drawbacks the law has, the way it is used by solicitors and barristers seems to work without us having to be unfriendly with each other. I do hope it continues that way for it would be totally unworkable if issues became so serious to make negotiations between lawyers unworkable.

In that case, all clients would be forced to go to Court and then we must trust absolutely that the Judge is independent, approachable and fair.

29. Past and Future Communications in Litigation

A lot is changing fast in communications between people. There are texts and emails where you don't have to talk to people face to face. Hardly any young people ring each other to have a chat. And there are videos, U tubes and more methods of communication I've never known about.

However, I'll keep to the subject of Law. In litigation, Advocacy was essential. In classical times, it was considered a very important skill to round off your education.

In my father's lifetime, Counsel were great advocates and gave speeches almost like classical times without any notes nor reading off a script. They never had notes in Classical times but just spoke off the cuff.

But is that all going to go?

Even presenters on television use the prompt as do politicians. But journalists in the field, the Foreign and War correspondents usually give their reports from no notes, running in trenches, followed by a crouching cameraman.

So what am I complaining about? About what might happen in the future.

I have a feeling Advocacy will slowly dwindle away. Why stand up and address a bench when you can sit at home and address a bench of Judges all in their homes, all from notes, out of sight on the desktop which can't be seen by the tiniest of cameras these days?

You can probably read from a script hovering out of sight and above your own screen, so it looks as if you are 'ad-libbing'.

Why not record all you are going to say, press a timed button and then go out? Alexa can speak for you. She may be able to field any questions bowled to her by the judges Alexas or Alexes (male or female).

The only reason I fear this is because humans are getting more and more used to addressing issues instantly, without thinking carefully about the reply and being logical.

Maybe the last frontier will be crossed when Artificial Intelligence will be used as judges, so they won't need to hear arguments… but surely, we will need a human to draft and pose the questions?

30. Mothers and Their Sons in Trouble

Attitudes to a wrongdoer within the family is a subject that one can discuss under the heading of legal, especially the attitude of Mothers to Sons.

If one takes the facts of any case and asks an independent observer to make a moral judgement of the behaviour of the wrongdoer, one would get an agreement as to culpability; however, if one switches to the Mother of the wrongdoer, especially if he is a male, an instant defensive attitude will he heard.

I suppose it's understandable but, in my career, I have seen facts and apportionment of blame being orally twisted by mothers in support of sons.

One type of case is divorce. When the son's marriage is going well, the mother is supportive of her daughter-in-law, because it coincides with her son's interests. As soon as the marriage breaks down, even where it is because of adultery by the son which, let's say, he hides from the wife, suddenly the mother wades in, says the breakdown has caused great distress to her son and the son in fact was driven to the adultery because of the daughter-in-law's fault.

Maybe that is in the nature of mothers, especially towards sons. Novels and fables have been written and talked about mothers and sons and their relationships ;but I am limiting my comments to my knowledge within the Practice of Law and litigation; it is probably not a good idea to call a mother to court to mitigate the son's behaviour.

I had a case of murder where a young man stabbed his girlfriend 15 times, was arrested, and admitted it in interview which lasted 2 days.

I went to see his mother who was middle-aged but disabled and I noticed, as soon as I entered her cottage, her desperate support of her son. I waited to see if she would plead some sort of defence of his actions as near as possible to defences in law. No, there was no self-defence; in fact he tried to kill himself after he had committed the murder, an action (not words) which acknowledged his guilt.

She was desperate to protect him, and I think was in denial of the facts. He was her son? Was that not enough for him to be acquitted? I found it difficult to handle her protestations.

Eventually, he said he had taken drugs so that he didn't know what he was doing; the medical and psychological reports did not support that and he was convicted of murder and given 15 years.

So, for the preservation of the species, mothers must continue to be protective of sons, but such protection will not stand up to legal scrutiny.

31. How Murderers Behave

When someone does wrong against the law, how do they feel or come to terms with what they have done.

If you are an opportunist, you will do wrong and gain from it and justify it either by saying you need to *gain*, and your need is bigger than the loser's loss.

Or you will justify your action by blaming the loser for being stupid enough to allow you to gain.

What if you cause violence to another? You may be in a temper and strike out. You might feel you were provoked; you might strike out in self-defence. In either case, you don't personally gain by causing hurt to someone else.

However, you might cause violence to steal from someone. You may need to inflict it to gain possession of something.

What of the worst crime of all? How do you behave or justify your action if you murder someone? If you do it to gain something, that gain must be very big, especially to take someone's life.

I will now give a real example that I had. My client stabbed his girlfriend 14 times. I have mentioned this before, but I haven't gone into detail as to how he then behaved.

The court didn't accept that he had Diminished Responsibility either because he was on drugs or was so provoked by his girlfriend—both situations would allow the charge of Murder to Manslaughter.

But he did actually behave. He behaved as if he had remorse. He tried to cut an artery in his leg and he started bleeding but he found he didn't die.

He scrawled on the wall in the bathroom: 'see you on the other side'.

Then his behaviour became more irrational. He filled the bath and tried to drown himself in it—how? By putting a television on top of him to weigh himself down in the water. That didn't work. Then he thought someone might be outside in the street 3 floors below so he threw a heavy object through the glass window and it landed heavily on the pavement.

So the police arrested him, took him to hospital and he survived and I was called to the Police Station.

So how do you square his behaviour—remorse, self-preservation, cowardice or what?

We shall never know but a lot of law-abiding citizens will always read about criminals and how inexplicably they behave, get arrested and then ask mitigation when in court. Is it just simply that they are cowards?

32. The Most Common Crime-Shoplifting

Statistics confirm that shoplifting is top of all statistics in crime. For instance, in America, one in 11 Americans have shoplifted. 55% of shoplifters started as teenagers and 25% of shoplifters are teenagers. You can look it all up but the statistics make it top of every question you care to ask.

Well, OK, what happens on the ground in my experience?

Most of my cases involved shoplifters and most of them stole items to sell to convert into cash to buy drugs. Most of my clients were on benefits which just wouldn't stretch to buying drugs.

Now, very occasionally, there was no explanation for shoplifting and in a lot of my cases to avoid a trial the client pleaded guilty, and no explanation was given to the sentencing court as to why he or she committed the crime. In one case, as I have said before, an old lady said she didn't mean to do it which immediately catapulted her into a trial situation which she did not want. It would attract publicity which she didn't want her husband to read about.

However, I'm sure I could have run a defence if I had employed a psychiatrist who might confirm the client was depressed, one symptom of which is to shoplift—to attract attention to the depression.

On the other side of the coin, stealing high-value goods was undertaken so they could be sold. In one case, my client stole a bottle of good brandy worth about £40. But he could only resell it to those, who would risk handling stolen goods, for about £5 to £10—not a good 'markup' or rather 'markdown'.

The real problem is how to define theft of small items from shops. After all, in the strict legal definition, the Prosecution have to be sure that the thief ***intended permanently to deprive the owner***. Maybe it should be treated in law as a special case. However, the owner might be upset if no charge was put when he or she had lost the item; but the thief got away with ***no action taken*** because they didn't mean to steal.

The answer eventually in all forms of theft was to develop safeguards to make it difficult to steal. Cameras sprouted all over shops and became clearer. Thieves were aware of this as one could view videos showing thieves looking all about and high up to see where cameras were.

Bottles of alcohol had anti-theft devices attached to the bottle. Some items caused alarms to go off if you went through to the exit without paying.

Just the same as cars; the law was no deterrent, but anti-theft devices did the trick. In fact, most shoplifters of small valueless items got hardly a sentence at all—no deterrent at all. The deterrent was also not the sentence once you did get caught.

Other ways of stealing clothes were to wear them under your other clothes. Once again, if something was attached to the clothes then the metal detector would go off if you went out without paying. However, what overtook that device was the selling of clothes by post which could be returned with no charge even though you wore it for one night.

I'm not sure what will stop or diminish shoplifting. It increases when a depression happens or when inflation put up the prices of goods. Maybe it will never be solved. It certainly won't be solved or diminished by a high sentence or good mitigation.

33. Paedophiles

The above word comes from the Greek meaning *child,* the first part of the word and the second part of the word meaning *loving, friendly, dear*; together the meaning is a sexual desire directed to children.

Now, talking of Greek in classical times, it was acceptable for adults in those times to have sexual relations with children and more often than not between adult men and boys. I merely mention this as an example of how morals and laws change through time and by different cultures.

Now, however, law has turned on its head and paedophilia is one of the most detestable of crimes, so much that it is more despised than other quite ordinary but despicable crimes, especially the most common—thefts of all sorts.

If someone is accused of such an offence, whether it is true or not, he'd better keep his head down as the general public might attack him if they knew where he lived before he has been acquitted by a jury of any wrongdoing.

Indeed, as I write, a woman under the age of consent, to all intents a child, accused a group of men of grooming her, assaulting her and raping her. She dealt with this in Facebook and got an enormous amount of support throughout her readers. A man she accused was arrested and refused bail. He was kept in prison and put in the Sex Offenders wing, even though he was refused bail after being charged.

Eventually, the police followed up his alibi—for he denied the charges. It was found she made up the accusations and eventually was put on trial herself for ***Perverting the course of justice*** and other crimes and was convicted.

Indeed, she even accused gangs of men of assaulting her and hit her face with a hammer to provide some visible evidence to support her false accusations of assault. She is due to be sentenced.

In another case, a professional man's address was attacked by a group of moral humbugs because his profession, as shown on his brass plate affixed to his business address, was as a *paediatrician*, a name also derived from the Greek word for child.

So we now have a class of crime which was most opportunistic, or used to be, in private boarding schools for boys, otherwise known as Preparatory schools. It seems that the crime was more prevalent between adult men and boys rather than between adult women and girls. I can't account for that.

In any event, there was more than ever opportunity for Paedophilia in Preparatory school run by men who were in authority as teachers, housemasters and headteachers—the Preparatory Schools usually accommodating boys under 12 to 13.

Referring to the case above about the woman who accused men of rape and assault when she was under age, the Prosecuting Authority seemed to be very willing to accept her account and charge the man maybe because she as the supposed victim was a woman.

On the same account, there was a case in a Preparatory school in Dorset where the master who eventually owned the school and was Headteacher was accused of Paedophilia. The police were informed but the parents never wanted to support a prosecution. It seemed to have been swept under the carpet and eventually he died of dementia in 2016 without ever having been brought to Court.

There was also a case of a master who was employed by a Preparatory school which served Eaton and one of the victims even wrote a book about it called *Stiff Upper Lip* by Alex Renton, also about an elite boarding school.

I highlight all this as an example through the ages of a behaviour which though once acceptable in Classical times was later an abhorrent crime, not to be mentioned.

Indeed, especially so in my Great-Grandfather's, Sir Edward Clarke, time who was a top barrister and who defended Oscar Wilde. Oscar Wilde was a accused of paedophilia. My great Grandfather defended him but never mentioned it in his Autobiography.

Just another example of types of crimes set on a special pedestal dictated by the Mores of the time.

34. Evidence by Identification

"Now who was it I was talking to the other day?"

or

"Who did I bump into the other day, I remember his face?"

or

"Now what was his name?"

or

"Where have I seen him somewhere before?"

or

"I'm sure it was so and so."

We all know these words we've said but we just can't quite remember, can't quite recall—memory?

Or we might have been to a party and recount something that has happened there. We are told by our listener that they were there too.

"Oh, were you there too, I didn't see you," comes the repost. We get a look as if our memory has gone wrong, how embarrassing.

The memory lets you down but what if you were in court and your memory lets you down?—that would be embarrassing.

I went on a course once and watched a video which is quite famous. You are shown a group of people playing basketball and throwing a ball to each other. Then suddenly and quietly, a person in a monkey suit walks through this group from left to right while they are still energetically playing.

The video stops, the lights are turned on and we are asked what was unusual about the video. Most people don't comment and then the man in the monkey suit is pointed out. We all look very embarrassed when the video is played back to us. How could we have ever missed that?

And so it is with witnesses. When they are at a scene of a crime, they are not expecting to notice anything in particular. After the event, they recount what they thought they saw but may not be able to describe the offender. They were not expecting to describe anyone. They were just going about their lawful business and concentrating on their destination.

The moral of this observation is ***do not rely on a witness's recounting of what he or she saw.***

Why? Because their mind is not expecting to have to do that. And that weakness is what Defendants rely on to get acquitted, the fallibility of a witness remembering what he saw.

The law knows this and that is why, for the sake of the defendant, identification parades are undertaken in the strictest impartiality.

And that is why **Dock Identification** would not be allowed. The witness is asked, "Do you see the person who did this or that in this courtroom?"

Of course, he's going to look to the forlorn person standing in the Dock, the Defendant accused, and say: "Yes, it was him."

When I first practised, identification was undertaken as it had been almost in Victorian times. The police went out into the street and asked people who looked like my client if they would come to the police station and stand in an identification parade. It was all a bit *hit and miss*. Maybe the member of the public didn't want to be picked out and maybe the police found it difficult to find volunteers. They were paid.

Things have progressed to more fairness. Now there is an enormous data of images of people, thousands, and you as a solicitor can pick who you want. The client does not have to go at all but his image is kept when he was first arrested.

The idea being that so long as the client agreed to an identification parade, it was his fault if he was picked out because his solicitor had picked the other 'lookalikes' in the parade.

Mind you, if the client didn't agree to have an identification parade, an adverse inference could be drawn against him and who wants the jury to know you refused to have an identification parade!

35. If You Lose a Case, Should You Resign, Like Sportsmen Do?

If you lose a case as an advocate, should you resign or go on a training course? Is it like sport where losing is a sign of failure? After all, you expected to win because you fully advised your client. If you didn't expect to win, your client would have pleaded guilty, or would he? However, he expected the truth to come out, but his truth is different from the real truth. Maybe he went against your advice and you have become a reluctant advocate.

How do laymen decide which litigator to choose? I must say I have never had to give details of how many cases I've won and lost—yet it had crept into CVs of surgeons showing whether their operations have been successful or not or whether their patient has died on the operating table.

I don't think that peculiar. What I think is peculiar is that litigators or advocates don't have to justify their existence by disclosing their wins and losses. My own experience is that you can't be judged by how many cases you win. Cases are not decided just by your advocacy but also by the expertise of the witness.

Your client or any one of your witnesses might let you down by their incoherence or, as they say in legal language, 'they do not come up to proof'.

The facts of the case may determine you have a lost case; but in that case, maybe your client in Criminal cases should plead guilty or settle a civil case before it goes to trial. It is true that there are excellent advocates, because they can convince Judges and Juries that their truth is the correct one and should be accepted.

But more often than not outside circumstances beyond the control of the advocate determine the result,

36. Reading Law Books Looking up the Law

Non-lawyers think of lawyers as 'learned'. Barristers are addressed in court as 'my learned friend'. Incidentally, they also address their opponent as 'friend' to avoid antagonistic hostility. The truth is, from my experience, the most law books and cases I read were at University—over 60 years ago.

Barristers do read law books and cases because they are asked to Advise in writing and those requesting Advice want sources.

But if the truth was known, solicitors are Practitioners rather than Researchers; the definition of a practitioner is ***a person actively engaged in an art, discipline or profession.***

So, looking at the definition, I am now not a practitioner because I am retired. I would like to tell my friends who ask Legal Advice, now I'm retired, that I am no longer a Practitioner. (Also, I am no longer insured).

Anyway, getting back to law books, I have never had to look up the Law as the Law on most of the problems I am presented with is self-evident. And if the Law is uncertain, it may either be because I don't practise in it which was usual years ago; or one didn't know the law (or it was not clear). The Gillick case back in 1985 was such a one, (which went all the way to the House of Lords). I don't think anyone knew what the Law was and wanted clarification from the highest court in the land.

Remember, litigation is costly and the riskiest thing about it is that if you sue the loser will have to pay the winner's costs. So, it's an expensive thing going to court.

As a practitioner, I do have standard practitioner's books I can skim through. Going to the Magistrates court, the very small handbook used by all solicitors is ***Blackstone's Magistrates Court handbook***; mine is dated 2013, the year I retired. You can slip it in your pocket and probably it was the last of the guides you could slip into your pocket before laptops were used, which will also have all the details the handbook had.

If you want the absolute guide for the Magistrate's court, I could take to court all three volumes of ***Stone's Justices Manual,*** All the volumes slipped into a plastic handbag with a handhold; however, as they were pretty heavy and the plastic split after a bit. You usually did your research back in the office and then photocopied the relevant pages to take to court. When you get to Higher courts, the bible for Criminal law can be found in the criminal law practitioner's bible, ***Archibald.*** It is coloured red.

You could borrow your colleague's books or even those belonging to the clerk.

However, all that paperwork has been overtaken by laptops and computers.

If you watch any modern law drama on film or television, shelves of lovely leather-bound law books would be illustrated in the background; that does not reflect reality.

Binding law books like the ***All England law books***, ***the Weekly law reports*** and others is very expensive. They can be seen online—what a revolution!

If you go to the Law courts, especially in the Strand in London, you may see clerks pushing trolleys of books and cardboard boxes of papers, but I suspect this habit is slowly diminishing. Barristers used to carrying bags in which they kept their gowns, wigs and books.

In the high court, the ***Supreme Court Practice*** is the bible, in several volumes, and in the County Court, the ***Green book*** was the thing.

The interesting thing is that Lord Justice Woolf reformed completely the practise in the ***County Court Practice*** to make it simpler; and so, the green book expanded in size and weight!

37. A Rape Case and My Brother

As I write, sexual offences against women are in the headlines under the banner headline of *'MeToo'*. It has always been a crime to sexually assault a woman, or man for that matter, but it was underlined, highlighted by the multitude of cases brought to light and pursued before the courts in America and Britain.

However, there was no such attention around when I had my first serious sexual case. It was just another sexual crime, though the most serious-***Rape.***

My client was a lorry driver and picked up a hitchhiker around the Midlands. He had sex with her, but she complained it was Rape and made a complaint to the police. So it was not a case of boyfriend/girlfriend and the question of whether she consented in that relationship.

My client was much older than the young victim. She said she was hitchhiking and got a lift from him but then he dumped her in a layby.

They are difficult cases and, of course, he could be telling the truth. In those days, the victim had no anonymity and had to give evidence in open court and not behind a screen.

How do you come to terms with the result of such a case? Before the result, maybe he was innocent and must be considered so. She would have to be cross-examined by my counsel, my brother, who was a young barrister at the time, and be accused of lying; for what purpose I don't know.

However, as soon he is found guilty, the truth is different. The truth is what the jury says it is—***beyond all reasonable doubt.***

Did I look at my client in a different light?

No, but it was difficult. He got 6 years and didn't appeal; There is no appeal unless there was some ***Miscarriage of Justice*** and there was none here; it was his word against hers. The prosecution had to prove the case and not the defence to disprove it.

The ironic postscript of this narrative is that my client served his sentence—he served half and went back to live with his wife.

A year or two later, he came to see me again. He was to be arrested for sexually assaulting another young girl in a country lane. He denied it.

I was wavering but I had to act for him. He seemed to trust me even though he had been convicted of the Rape case.

Eventually, to his benefit the prosecution dropped the case as there was not enough evidence to proceed to a court case. They knew his previous conviction as I did.

I was mildly surprised but carried on acting for Criminals for the next 20 years even though a lot of them I didn't believe.

38. Serendipity in the Legal Family

Serendipity is defined as *"the faculty or phenomenon of finding valuable or agreeable things not sought for"*.

Does everyone have serendipity or just lawyers in our family.

On the 27th December 1979 our son Thomas was born. On the same day my stepbrother (now a judge – see the previous chapter when he was a barrister) had a son they called Edward.

My father who was then a judge was thrilled and put both births in the Times personal column.

His Honour Judge Peter Clarke Q.C and his son (my nephew)

Well alright that was pretty unusual. In Houston I was in a hotel on holiday, and I was standing in front of a lift. The lift opened and there was a barrister who I used regularly and in particular the case in my last book when a relative was run down on a zebra crossing and which I also refer to it in chapter 9 about Terrifying judges.

What about a third time? Surely not. On the 14th May this year, I was sitting on a station called Sestri Levante on the Italian Riviera. Sitting beside me was a woman who spoke English. To be sociable I asked her where she came from, and she said Hampshire. I said I had a stepbrother called Peter Clarke who lived in Bramley. She replied "I used to live in Bramley and my best friend if his wife Vicky Clarke."

What can I say?

The lady sitting on the Sestri Levanti station

39. How I Got Paid Over the Years

I have always suffered from the comments:

"You're a solicitor so you are alright."

or

"Why not retire early—lawyers always have a bit put away."

I understand in Sweden, people's pay is public knowledge. Everyone knows what his or her neighbour earns.

It'll never happen in Britain but now that I'm retired, I have decided to show what I earned throughout my 44 years. It might be boring, it might be illuminating but at least it will allow the readers to make up their own minds whether I did earn 'loads of money' on legal aid or not.

Initially, I was an articled clerk and I suppose if minimum pay existed in 1970, I would have been paid that. But at the time, it was considered that the firm was training me, so I ought to get less. So in my first year, I got £560 a year (or £10 a week) and I was paid monthly.

I should hasten to say that prior to my generation training as a lawyer, previously Articled clerks would have to pay a lump sum to be articled. However, back in 1970, the unions were up in arms going on strike and demanding more pay to keep up with inflation. We heard that and read the papers and eventually after one year, our pay went up to £760 a year, a pay rise of 36%-unheard of nowadays.

After that, as I changed firms, my pay went up. That was the only way to get a pay rise as firms got frightened of the escalator of pay rises. So solicitors were always expensive but their charges bore no relation to the pay of the staff. The Partners wanted a profit if they were to stay in business.

Well, my pay throughout the years carried on till I became a partner in 2001. Suddenly, one can see an enormous increase. The year before I earned £36,000 as an employee—as a partner, I earned £76,000 in my first year.

However, I continued to do Legal Aid work which didn't pay much. That meant the other partners who were raking it in doing non-legal aid work were subsidising my efforts even though I worked hard. My rate of income from work was much less than private work, possibly 60% less.

So the firm gave up Legal Aid work and I moved on to another firm.

Then a different type of pay became the norm. You got a basic pay which was quite low but as an incentive, you had a target for net costs (net of vat and disbursements). If you reached that target, you were given a bonus of 20% of the fees over, say, £70,000 (if that was your target).

It certainly made you work hard and get clients where you can, sometimes at the expense of other earners in the same firm. For if you strived like mad and on the last day of the end of the accounting year, you got £69,999 (work in progress), it didn't count. No bonus and you had to start all over again.

No wonder you took calls from the police station on Saturday and Sunday and on holiday. If you didn't take the client, someone else in the firm would or a fee earner in another firm. On this system, there was no overtime paid—the bonus was everything.

Finally, I went part-time before I retired and my pay was reduced pro rata. Legal Aid still didn't pay and I took a reduction in pay a year before I retired. On my last year, I was earning £15,000—so not really rolling in it but having said that, Legal Aid clients, dealing with Prisoners and the courts was far more interesting than conveyancing and chasing private divorce clients for their money

40. Advising Even After I've Retired!

My father told me "…people will want to bend your ear about their legal problems at any time and any place."

Based on this assertion, I somehow thought clients would just fall in my lap. However, it wasn't quite like that. I sat in my first office and waited but they didn't really come. I somehow got the idea that the people who came to you would be your friends and neighbours, but it didn't quite happen like that.

Throughout my career, clients came in because they had problems that my friends never had—burglars, thieves, etc. the criminal lot.

As I've said before, I didn't act for my father or wind up my mother's estate—nor my son's divorce. But both while practising and especially after I retired, friends would sidle up to me, ring me up, pop into my house; after saying hello, the conversation usually went like this:

Me: "Hello X, how nice to hear from you."

X: "Hello John, are you well—tell me how is your son getting on?"

Me: "Alright."

(Waiting to find out what he wanted)

"How's business?"

"Alright."

We went on circling each other so we got to know each other's families and their health perfectly. I thought I'd bring it to an end.

Me: "Nice to hear from you, X… we must get in touch."

X: "Oh yes, John, I almost forgot to mention…"

And out comes the problem. The introductions at the beginning of the phone call lasted say 10 minutes and discussing the problems lasted about an hour. I didn't give advice, but I should have said that I'm not insured. The caller never actually asked advice but would pose his problem and then waited to see what I might say.

After an hour, I had to escape somehow so I might say:

"Nice to hear from you, X, I think that's the doorbell…"
Or

"Whoops, my wife has just told me tea is ready. I'd better ring off…"

Or

"I'd better ring off as we have to get to the theatre we've booked."

I know Lawyers are thought to be expensive and people are reluctant to come into the office when I was practising and pay money. What galls me most is when a friend would ring, go through all the introductions, and then ask if I could ring his friend because he's in a hell of a state about his divorce/son's problem/ wife's problem/ his own problem.

Fool as I was, I ring the friend, at my own cost, silently listen to all his problems, mumble some comments and then it slips out that he has a solicitor and merely wanted a second opinion.

You don't stop working even after you have retired and are uninsured.

I had a friend from way back in the smallholding days. He worked on the same farm as I did and when I moved to the West Country on my retirement, he lived in Devon and said we ought to get together for a chat. He suggested that, not me. I didn't see any danger signals He travelled to Somerset, and we went to the pub.

We talked about the old times and then I asked him about his property. And did he talk; I should have realised that. He'd bought a smallholding and his eyes lit up.

"You see," he said, "we have a field down a lane. And my neighbour,"—here we go, I thought; why did I ask that question?—"My neighbour thinks he can go down this track, which he can't." Then he added with more gusto, "Look, I'll draw a plan" and he got a bit of old paper from his pocket and started drawing a plan.

I tried to look interested but that only encouraged him.

He went on and on and my drink stood in front of me untouched. It was time to go. The pub was about to close.

"Look," he said at our parting, "I'll photocopy my deeds and send them to you. Then you can come over to my place and you'll be able to see for yourself, on the ground so to speak."

I nodded as I waved goodbye to him. I didn't manage to slip in that as I was retired and uninsured, I would not be covered for giving legal advice, but it was too late—he had gone.

41. The Law, Lawyers and Activists

I'm not sure if it's a criticism of me or not but I'm not an Activist. Surely, people might say, all Lawyers must be activists. You must believe in things for your whole ***raison d'etre*** is to expound a client's ideals and beliefs.

Yes, my client's, not mine.

In fact, I get frightened by Activists who shove their ideals down your throat. I suppose I can do it for someone else but for all I know, I might sound very unconvincing. I leave that to any audience who might hear me. I did win some cases.

My wife says I don't believe in any belief I expound. you **'argue for the sake of it'.** Being Devil's advocate.

I think I have been corrupted by being able, and indeed required to take on any point of view that I am asked to do, for money. Even though I am retired I have got into the habit of taking the contrary view. That doesn't mean I want to argue serious points; I back away from them for fear of offending my opponent. So, it's due to fear that I'm not an Activist, and also because I am a coward.

In a Courtroom, you take on an argument without anyone being rude at you or to you. There are rules of politeness and you don't have to be emotional—you are not on stage.

Nowadays, as I've said before, lots of advocates read dryly from scripts without any emotion. However, I may be getting into the minority.

Advocates and lawyers more and more believe in what they argue. Lucky I've retired and so am old-fashioned. I have the luxury of watching others argue.

In court I am merely promoting the argument that the law supports my client's view. The law or idea of right and wrong is fixed before I even walked into court for my Client. I am just asking the court to determine what the law is.

This, of course, is very surprising. Parliament, our voted representatives, passed the Law so we should know what it means. You just have to pose to me the questions, "Then why are lawyers ever needed, ever since Romans times and before?" Drafters of legislation are never clear what they mean.

42. New Ways to Get Legal Advice and Representation

What of the future? Is there a revolution going on somewhere that I don't know about?

Well, first, the division between barristers and solicitors.

When I was practising, if you wanted a barrister to act for you in Court, you had to get a solicitor.

Now for the first time, you can look up the internet and find a barrister who will give you a quote directly. It's a new process and a slow one but that is a real revolution.

There are minor changes which are not revolutionary. No wigs in court, no gowns. That is going to be difficult as the Lawyer's clubs like their dress code though they don't have it in America; nor do they have the division between high street lawyers and advocates.

You have the same system in medicine. You can't go to a consultant directly. You can now get advice over the phone when you dial 101. Maybe you should ring some sort of ***artificial intelligence*** to get Legal Advice—who knows. They do accumulate data and knowledge as we know so they learn. You can feed into these robots, and they get better at telling you the answers.

So, no division between barristers and solicitors, no gowns. Initial advice from a robot.

When I was practising you could get any advice on English law on Legal Aid. Maybe what will replace Legal Aid in ***Artificial intelligent machines.***

After all, we are always discerning new things about the body and ways of curing new pandemics; so medicine changes as do diseases.

Surely then, if law is man made and written down, how much simpler would it be to get ***artificial intelligence*** to answer legal man made problems?

43. My Reputation as a Lawyer

I stand in an imaginary cocktail party, though they don't happen these days. Someone approaches me trying to chat me up.

"And what do you do?"

I look down in my glass, trying to disown what I am about to say.

"I am a solicitor."

There is silence and the onlooker tries to think of something nice to say. It's like someone says that they are in computers. It's a conversation-stopper.

Now the silence is not because the questioner does not know about lawyers. They probably know a lot about lawyers and it's not good. You read Dickens; can you find anything in all his books that is good about lawyers?

None.

People get frightened when they speak to lawyers wondering whether they are going to be quoted, have a statement taken down about what they say or sued on that.

They don't say, "Oh how terrible" or "What a low-paid job," or "However do you survive?" None of these sympathetic exclamations are made.

It gets worse if the questioner, out of politeness, persists. Maybe this is a lawyer who has some redemptive qualities. "What sort of law do you practise?"

I answer, "Criminal Law."

There is silence. How do you persist when someone acts for crooks? Let's see, maybe he acts for innocent people.

"Oh, I see; when someone is innocent and needs defending; it could be you or me."

I think about that line of questioning. My reputation is slowly sinking like the Titanic, but I can't be dishonest. "Well, not in all cases. I act for prisoners who have been convicted as well."

The conversation dwindles to a trickle.

So, at best, the cocktail hand plus glass moves to my female neighbour. They have won points already by being females. The score so far is minus 10 to me, plus 50 to my neighbour.

Then the questioning continues, "And what do you do?" the female is asked.

"I am a nurse." I throw my racket in the ring and concede the set. I've lost the match.

I really should have lied and said I was a female, a nurse or carer and I also would have won the point, set and match.

44. The Law and Practice of the New Morality—The Environment and Climate Change

This is a memoir of a lawyer who has retired and so is out of date. However, I can say what was important in law and practice in my day and whether there should now be a change.

Some people think the most important issue, these days as I write, is the Environment and Climate Change. Some people think the *only* important issue is the Environment and Climate change and all others are just putting their heads in the sand.

During the short time I have practised, namely 44 years, the worst crimes were either to do with injury to your fellow man by Common Assault, Grievous Bodily Harm *(G.B.H.)*, and Murder; and protection of property, Theft, Burglary Robbery (a combination of projection of humans from injury and protection of property).

Initially, the only persons who were recognised in law were men and the head of the family, the **Pater Familias** in classical times. Slaves and females were not recognised. Then ships were recognised as entities to be protected by law. Slaves were then recognised and given legal rights as persons.

At the end of the 19th century, railroads were treated as legal entities like people.

In Victorian times, corporations were recognised as legal entities. In the next century, women got the vote and were protected by law.

The big change around the world today is that natural features are now recognised and protected just like people were. In New Zealand, certain rivers, lakes and forests are given protection as if they were people, and the same is happening in Ecuador, Lake Erie in Canada and even the Taj Mahal.

Humans can act as trustees for these natural objects and places and bring cases in court for them on their behalf.

So in law, in reality the environment is getting protected. Most practice happens every day in the Magistrate's Court and more so than all civil law.

Maybe the law ought to change to protecting the Environment and concentrate on climate change enforcement. Maybe prosecutions should concentrate on protecting the Environment and the atmosphere.

What about the practice of law; going to court and arguing in a central place is the main activity of litigation.

Maybe we should all be at home practising law and not travelling about. Maybe the Law Court as a place should be made redundant.

At this stage, maybe we should continue to have Judges and Judgements, but they should stay at home and view each other on Zoom. The pandemic was quite good practice for such behaviour. In fact, I think there are statistics for proving that the pandemic lockdown was excellent for the environment. Maybe we should learn from that.

Ironically, it was the pandemic that reduced travelling in the law. Prisoners were kept in prison and they appeared at court by closed circuit viewing. We didn't realise it at the time but that helped the climate more than anything else.

That was not the purpose. The initial purpose was to avoid the disruption of waiting for prisoners to arrive at Court. A lot of time, they just didn't arrive and judges exploded at the ensuing disruption. Let's trade on that success for the sake of the Environment.

I also repeat that some law litigation, judgments and advice could be dealt with by ***Artificial Intelligence***. We have Law and it must be enforced as history has taught us; otherwise, you have chaos. Technology however has expanded at a pace that might indicate a different way of delivering it, especially considering the new most important morality of the day—the environment.

The demand for change is not new. Travelling around is not good for the environment. Back in the Middle Ages through to the 18th century, religion and power were considered by the law worthy of protection. Now, it might be the environment that now needs protecting, otherwise the whole world is doomed!

45. Closing Courts

Near the end of my career in the courts, suddenly there was a proposal that my local magistrates court was earmarked to close—and we thought they would go on and on; how wrong we were.

OK, supermarkets and stores close and go bust; Woolworths closed during my career and that was a shock. New ones are invented. But that is business: they must pay their way.

But surely justice does not have to pay its way. It has been there since Magna Carta. But we underestimated that someone must pay for it being run.

The party in charge however thought otherwise and one of the first trench of cuts was my local Magistrates Court. Once we had all recovered from our shock, we gathered the Justices before we represented our clients and ourselves the solicitors.

The criminals were oblivious of what could happen to them. They would have to catch the bus to another magistrate's court 20 miles away to the east or west of the town. We made representations to the Ministry far away in London. We mentioned our clients would not turn up at court and there would be more government costs in getting them and bringing them to court. Or they might even steal a car; they certainly wouldn't catch a bus. The bus service was abysmal.

The cleverest criminals would ring the court to say they'd be late and come in the afternoon. Would the court allow that?

Well, we stuck together and for some reason, our arguments were heard, and they didn't close the court—but closed another in another part of the county.

We breathed a sigh of relief.

2 years later, the Ministry tried closing it again. This time they chose the summer months to announce it and gave those objecting 28 days to make representations. We had no fight left and the court was closed. I could no longer walk across from my office and enter the court 20 yards away, just in time for the first case to be called. I had to travel the 20 miles one way or the other and Legal Aid would have to pay my travelling and parking costs.

However, that was not the end. I would have to travel to the nearby Magistrate's court but then that was decided to be closed. A beautiful court purpose-built in the 1950s lined with American oak panelling with cost no object—all closed only fit for a court stage set for the films. I understand it is still closed and no film has been filmed there.

No one was absolved from these cuts. My brother was a Judge at Blackfriars court in London and that was also closed just before he retired.

46. Technology in Solicitors' Offices Over 44 Years

As I said in the first chapter of my first book, my first firm in 1970 had a telephone exchange with plug-in connections joining incoming calls to those within the firm.

Dictaphones were enormous, the size of bricks, and no mobile phones. All older partners not used to these brick phones dictated to their personal secretaries orally, not touching any machines. The secretaries, all women, had huge typewriters and carriages which needed muscly women to yank them along to get to the next line. But all this was normal in 1970.

Later, Dictaphones got smaller, almost pocket-size, and the older partners retired and missed the progression which never stopped. Ordinary typewriters were changed to electric typewriters and finally computers came along in 1990.

When I left, I had a secretary but afterwards, letters and other correspondence and documents were dictated by the fee earner at his or her own desk and it was picked up by a room of secretaries some miles away and automatically typed on a computer and sent off. The fee earner never saw the letter. It was signed electronically for the distant secretaries were told orally exactly what standard format the letter should be given.

And so, as I left, the space age came. Mobile phones progressed to iPhone on which you can do anything. Photographs could be taken of anything and transmitted to letters and attached—a mile away from the office that I entered in September 1970.

What will be the future?

47. How Can I Give a Picture of What the Legal Social Culture Was at the Time?

I have now left the law some time. I have not practised for some 11 years. Someone asked me, "You talk about people with wing collars; what were lawyers really like; how did they behave to each other and to clients?"

You can do no better than watch **Leo McKern's wonderful portrayal** in Michael Mansfield QC's stories of **Rumpole of the Bailey.**

-------------------------oOo---------------------